The Fearless Freelancer
How to Thrive in a Recession

Lori De Milto

PRINT ISBN: 978-1-64718-795-8
EPUB ISBN: 978-1-64718-796-5
MOBI ISBN: 978-1-64718-797-2

Published by BookLocker.com, Inc., St. Petersburg, Florida.

Printed on acid-free paper.

Booklocker.com, Inc.
2020

First Edition

Dedication

To my husband Julian De Milto, who has always believed in me.

Acknowledgments

I had a lot of help in developing this book and would like to thank:

Brian Corchiolo, visual-graphic designer/web developer, bpc Creative, who designed the book cover

Kathleen Labonge, MBA, freelance medical copyeditor, Write Point Editing Solutions, who edited the book

All of the freelancers who helped me choose the title and the cover, provided feedback to improve the book, and reviewed the book.

Reader Reviews of *The Fearless Freelancer: How to Thrive in a Recession*

"Finally—a book about how to recession-proof your business that is written especially for freelancers! *The Fearless Freelancer* is a must-read for anyone who wants to protect—and even grow—their business during challenging times. It's packed with tips that every freelancer can use to succeed in a recession."

Kristin Harper, PhD, MPH, ELS
Owner, Harper Health & Science Communications

"The Mighty Marketer strikes again! Armed with her personal experience from two previous recessions, Lori shows you how to survive and thrive during these uncertain times. There is no doubt that Lori is the freelance marketing expert."

Christina Sanguinetti, BMSc
Freelance medical writer

"Lori has written a soup-to-nuts guide to thriving as a freelancer, even in an economic downturn. She'll help you identify prospects who will pay you what your work is worth and guide you through the mechanics of contacting prospects, including sample email templates to use in marketing. She'll help you create the habit of regular marketing, using your natural work and focus rhythms to maximize productivity."

Joy Drohan, MS
Freelance writer and editor in environmental science

"This book can help every freelancer thrive during the recession, especially newbies. This is one of the books I wish I had during my early freelance career."

Ekaphan Ardharn
English to Thai finance translator

"What can freelancers do to thrive in a recession? Stay calm, find ways to stand out, and spend time marketing. The steps Lori outlines are clear and specific, and her tone is supportive and helpful. Freelancers will turn to this book for guidance throughout their careers."

Jennifer Holmes, ELS
Freelance medical editor

"No matter where you are in your career or what you're doing right or wrong, there is a lot for you here. There's resource-laden, real-world, practical advice with a healthy dose of inspiration. Even during these times, the word 'marketing' no longer strikes fear in my heart!"

Stan Sack, MD
Freelance Medical Writer, Pediatrician

"Lori makes the steps to thriving in a recession straightforward and easy to apply for any freelancer who is willing to put in the work. This is book is a must-have for any freelancer."

Mia DeFino, MS, ELS
DeFino Consulting, LLC
Freelance medical and science writer

"*The Fearless Freelancer* is an easy-to-read step-by-step guide to finding, marketing, and maintaining clients. Lori provides great tips about how find and attract reliable, high-paying clients even during the recession. This should be on every freelancer's 'must-read' book list to help him/her stay relevant in today's economy."

Katie Estes, PhD
Freelance Medical Writer

"*The Fearless Freelancer* is a motivational page-turner. This book has excellent and time-tested advice for new and experienced freelancers. You're bound to thrive and succeed if you have the right approach and follow Lori's expert advice offered throughout the book."

Kalpana Shankar, Ph.D.
Freelance medical and science writer

"Lori De Milto has created a tool that is engaging and practical for freelancers everywhere. Suited for both novice and veteran, *The Fearless Freelancer* has the nuts and bolts for standing out from the crowd and building success. The key takeaways were vital in allowing me to implement much of her guidance immediately. Bravo!"

Julie Nyhus MSN, FNP-BC
Health and medical writer

"At the height of the COVID-19 crisis, the timing of this book is perfect for any freelance writer. By applying Lori's thoughtful and professional advice, a writer can not only survive this recession, they can thrive. Lori's ability to inject hope into the practical information she provides is so welcome right now."

Lynelle Martinez, MBA
Lynelle Martinez Consulting, LLC
Freelance medical and technical writer

"I would recommend *The Fearless Freelancer: How to Thrive in a Recession* to any freelancer navigating the economic changes brought on by the COVID-19 pandemic. Lori is part instructor, part motivational coach, and she provides clear step-by-step instructions for marketing a freelance business as well as the encouragement to actually do it."

Erik MacLaren, PhD
Freelance Medical Writer

"*The Fearless Freelancer* is a survival guide for freelancers at all stages of their careers looking to grow their business and thrive during these uncertain times. Lori's actionable advice on developing your brand, finding ideal clients, and marketing your business will set you up for success now and into the future."

Vicki VanArsdale, MS
Freelance medical writer

"As a freelancer in my first year of business, I'm always looking to increase my client base and grow my income, regardless of economic conditions. *The Fearless Freelancer: How to Thrive in a Recession* lays out a clear, simple, and effective framework I can act on now to grow my freelance business during rough times."

Austin Ulrich, PharmD
Freelance medical writer

"It can be easy to get discouraged when everyone is talking about a down economy and high unemployment. However—and especially in a tough economy—companies need the help of strong freelancers to keep their businesses thriving. In her new book, *The Fearless Freelancer*, Lori De Milto offers an abundance of effective, forward-looking strategies to help freelancers stay positive, tailor their messages, and attract good clients."

Lisa Baker, PhD, CMPP
Freelance medical writer

"*The Fearless Freelancer* is essential reading during the COVID-19 recession. Its actionable steps provided in digestible nuggets avoid overwhelm. Lori's method works—even in this contracting economy—for freelancers who take the time to follow her suggestions."

Suzanne Bujara
Freelance medical writer

"Freelancing can seem like a daunting choice, especially for those without marketing experience. Worthy of its title, *The Fearless Freelancer* has provided me with concrete, well-detailed steps that I have found worthwhile for my own business. Useful examples and easy-to-understand advice make this book valuable for both current and aspiring freelancers during a recession."

Shilpa Shenvi
Freelance Medical Copyeditor

"A freelancer's goldmine is how I would describe *The Fearless Freelancer: How to thrive in a recession*. With her straightforward tell-it-as-it-is approach, Lori lays out a 10-step approach for success based on her personal experience that has kept her freelance business thriving despite multiple recessions. Packed full of practical ready-to-implement examples and bonus resources, this book is written with freelancers in mind, whether aspiring, just staring out, or neck deep with experience, to help you to succeed and thrive. This book will prepare you mentally, especially during an economic downturn, to be a fearless freelancer, but you will need to put into practice the advice Lori provides to see the results."

Helen Fosam, PhD
President, The Edge Medical Writing

"*The Fearless Freelancer* is a great follow-up to Lori's previous book, *7 Steps to High-Income Freelancing*. The new content is especially timely and relevant to the current world situation. It includes ways to incorporate sound marketing practices into everyday habits, enabling freelancers to maintain thriving businesses during challenging economic times."

Kathleen Labonge, MBA
Freelance medical copyeditor

"I have been freelancing for about 15 years, and my fear now comes from constantly needing to turn away new projects (which is also hard)! Lori truly inspires, because her steps are basic and simple--they are exactly what worked for me when I was building my business and more. I learned new things reading this book and highly recommend it. I also agree with Lori that you will become a successful and fearless freelancer if you follow her steps!

Jill W. Roberts, MS
Freelance Scientific Medical Writer

"Lori De Milto's new book, *The Fearless Freelancer*, is a good step-by-step overview of how to market yourself both during the coronavirus pandemic and afterwards. It gives very practical hands-on advice for how to use email, LinkedIn, and your own website to obtain new clients. However, if you're looking for advice on how to charge and get paid, how to run a business, or how to do your own accounting, you will need to look elsewhere."

Netanya Y. Spencer, MD, PhD
Scientific Writer

"The overriding message of *The Fearless Freelancer: How to Thrive in a Recession* is 'give more than you take.' That is Lori's secret recipe to thrive in a recession or any other time."

Mary Y. Nishikawa, MA, ELS
Publications Professional, CTD Consultant, and Protocol Writer

Table of Contents

10 STEPS TO FEARLESS FREELANCING IN A RECESSION

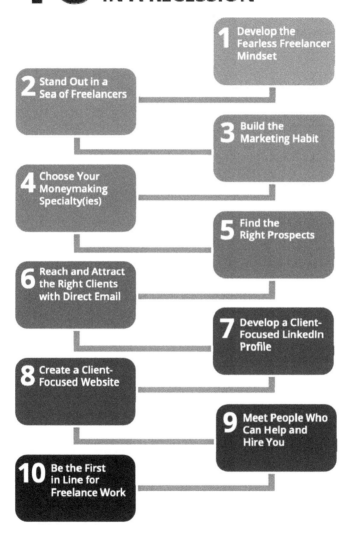

1 Develop the Fearless Freelancer Mindset

2 Stand Out in a Sea of Freelancers

3 Build the Marketing Habit

4 Choose Your Moneymaking Specialty(ies)

5 Find the Right Prospects

6 Reach and Attract the Right Clients with Direct Email

7 Develop a Client-Focused LinkedIn Profile

8 Create a Client-Focused Website

9 Meet People Who Can Help and Hire You

10 Be the First in Line for Freelance Work

Yes, You Can Thrive in a Recession!

"Action is the foundational key to all success."
— Pablo Picasso

If you're like most freelancers, you lost a little, some, or a lot of freelance work because of the COVID-19 pandemic. Now that the pandemic has led to the COVID-19 recession, things will get worse before they get better.

Steady, high-paying clients who need the help of talented freelancers are still out there. But there will be less work and more competition.

If you want to get your share of the available freelance work, you need to believe in yourself, adapt to the new normal, and take the right actions. Before I show you how to do these things, here's a brief overview of what's happening in the economy.

The Rise and Fall of the Economy

Just as a balloon rises and falls, so does the economy. Recessions are a natural part of the business cycle. I'm not an economist, but I'll try to explain what happens during a recession and how the COVID-19 recession is likely to impact freelancers.

Usually a recession happens after the economy has grown as much as it can. Then the economy starts to contract. At a certain point, the contraction becomes a recession.

The National Bureau of Economic Research defines a recession as "a significant decline in economic activity spread across the economy, lasting more than a few months." A more traditional definition of a recession is two quarters in a row of contraction in gross domestic product (the total value of goods and services made within a country during a period of time).

Some of us were freelancing during the Great Recession, from December 2007 to June 2009. This was the longest recession since the Great Depression. Before that, we had the 9/11 recession, from March to November 2001. Since the 1990s, the average recession in the U.S. has lasted 11 months.

A Different Type of Recession

But the COVID-19 recession is different than "normal" recessions. It happened and spread really fast, just like the pandemic. And this recession is global.

No one knows how long the COVID-19 recession will last or how bad it will be. How well the U.S. and the world manage the pandemic will play a big role in what happens next. Adequate testing, effective treatments, and a vaccine will all help economies recover. In the U.S., the economic stimulus package is helping. And the steep increase in unemployment may be temporary.

Social distancing and other extreme measures make normal life seem like a distant memory. Many of us have spouses/significant others and/or kids at home. Some of our spouses/significant others are unemployed. Our days are disrupted, and our loved ones need more of our time.

Stress and anxiety are sky-high. Focusing on freelancing is harder now—at a time when we need to be able to focus more on our businesses.

Become a Fearless Freelancer

While we can't make the recession go away or change the surreal circumstances of our daily lives, we can choose how we react. You can:

- Give in to panic and give up
- Ride out the recession and hope things get better
- Carry on and become a fearless freelancer.

If you panic and sit around feeling sorry for yourself, things will only get worse. If you try to ride out the recession, your freelance business may survive. Then again, it may not—because hope isn't a strategy.

But if you carry on, you can become a fearless freelancer—and thrive. Becoming a fearless freelancer means:

- Using a growth mindset
- Adapting to the new normal
- Taking the right actions.

Do the Right Marketing

Successful freelancers aren't smarter or more talented than freelancers who struggle. The difference is that we don't sit around hoping that clients find us. We don't rely on low-paying, high-competition freelance job sites and content mills. Instead, we go out and find the steady, high-paying clients we deserve through our marketing.

Taking the right actions means developing client-focused marketing tools and then consistently marketing your freelance business.

Doing this got me through the Great Recession and the 9/11 recession. The marketing that I did when I started my business let me become a 6-figure freelancer in 18 months. And the work I did back then—along with consistent but less intensive marketing since then—enabled me to thrive during two recessions.

During the Great Recession, I was so busy with client work that I barely noticed the economic downturn. And I don't think I even knew we had a recession in 2001.

The COVID-19 recession is my third recession. So far, I've seen an increase in business (as of August 2020 when this book went to press). But I know that if I do lose freelance work due to the recession, I can get more by doing more marketing.

Some Advice for New Freelancers

Did you know that freelancing is more stable than having a job? If you lose a job, it can be really difficult to get another one—especially in a recession. If you lose a client or some freelance work from a client, you have other clients and other freelance work. And it's much easier to get a new client or more work from a current client than it is to get a new job.

But if you've been freelancing less than a year or two or are starting your freelance business during the recession, it will be harder than it usually is to build a stable, successful freelance business. You can still do this, but you'll have to work harder and it will take you longer.

Also, you'll probably have to work for lower-paying, usually smaller, clients than more experienced freelancers. That's what most new freelancers do even in good times. But if you follow the steps in this book, you won't have to work for bad clients who pay ridiculously low fees.

See the information for new freelancers throughout the book.

Use a Proven Process

In *The Fearless Freelancer,* I share the secrets to my proven freelance marketing process for getting steady, high-paying clients—even in a recession. You will have to work hard. But you won't waste your time or effort because my process is based on what works best for freelancers.

And most of the work—developing your marketing foundation—will last for the rest of your freelance career. You will need to update your marketing messages, LinkedIn profile, and website as your business evolves or your specialty(ies) changes. But it's much easier to do updates than it is to develop your marketing foundation.

Adapt to the New Normal

If you've read my earlier book, *7 Steps to High-Income Freelancing* (2017), you'll see that much of the content in *The Fearless Freelancer* is similar. That's because the same basic principles work in good times and in bad. But there are a few differences.

In a recession and whatever the new normal turns out to be, what you think—your mindset—is as important as what you do. So Step 1 is about developing the fearless freelancer mindset. There are two more things that you must do if you want to thrive:

- Stand out from the competition
- Consistently market your freelance business.

Step 2 is about standing out in a sea of freelancers with your brand. Step 3 is about building the freelance marketing habit so that marketing becomes almost as easy as tying your shoes. The other seven steps are the same as in my earlier book, with a lot of updated information.

At the end of the book you'll find bonus content with links to more than two dozen checklists, templates, other tools, and blog posts.

Create a Stable, Successful Freelance Business

Despite the recession, you can get steady, high-paying clients and build a stable, successful freelance business. This book shows you what you need to do and how to do it. If you're willing to work hard, you can start to see changes in just a few months!

Ready to get started?

Step 1. Develop the Fearless Freelancer Mindset

"Let me tell you the secret that has led me to my goal.
My strength lies solely in my tenacity."
— Louis Pasteur

Thrive with the Right Mindset

What you think—your mindset—is just as important in what happens to your freelance business during the recession as what you do. In Step 1, you'll learn how to:

- Build your confidence and use a growth mindset to thrive in the recession
- Grow your grit and build your resilience to become a fearless freelancer
- Keep calm so you can keep anxiety at bay and focus on your freelance business.

Use a Growth Mindset

Freelancers who thrive in the recession won't be luckier or smarter than freelancers who struggle or fail. But they will have a growth mindset, grit, and resilience.

If you have a growth mindset, you believe that you can change your freelance future by learning new things, being persistent, and taking the right actions. You'll be willing to work hard to reach your goals.

But if you have a fixed mindset, you believe that your future is set in stone. And you may believe that you shouldn't have to work hard to succeed as a freelancer. Since doing better is beyond your control and you expect success to come to you without effort, you'll give up.

Become a Fearless Freelancer

You can build a growth mindset and become a fearless freelancer. Grit and resilience will help you do this. And you can grow your grit and build your resilience.

Grow Your Grit

Also called determination, mental toughness, or tenacity, grit is having the perseverance and passion to stick with your long-term goals until you reach them. Grit is carrying on even when you make mistakes or don't feel like you're making progress.

Remember how Charlie Brown kept trying to kick that football even though Lucy pulled it away from him every time? Charlie Brown never gave up. He had grit.

How successful we are is largely dependent on grit, says Angela Duckworth, a researcher at the University of Pennsylvania and author of the New York Times bestseller *Grit: The Power of Passion and Perseverance.* Duckworth's research shows that people with grit, when compared to others:

- Work harder to achieve goals
- Are happier
- Tend to be optimistic
- Are more resilient.

Build Your Resilience

While grit is something we always need, resilience helps us when bad things happen—like a recession. Resilience is the ability to meet adversity head-on, adapt, bounce back, and keep trying.

Most people aren't born resilient. Instead, they build resilience over time. If you consider adversity a challenge and deal with it, you'll become more resilient. But if you consider adversity a threat, you'll become less resilient.

How to Grow Your Grit and Build Your Resilience

Here are some says to grow your grit and build your resilience.

Be Positive

A negative attitude zaps your energy. And no one likes to be around—or work with—negative people. The recession will pass, just like all past recessions have. Believe in yourself and your ability to turn the challenges you're facing into opportunities. You have the power to make your freelance future brighter.

Take Action

Positive thinking alone isn't enough. You need to take action. Each action you complete is a small win. And each small win builds your confidence and motivates you to keep taking action.

Finishing this chapter is a small win. Finishing the entire book is a bigger small win. Taking the actions in all of the steps in the book is a big win that will help you get the steady, high-paying clients you deserve.

Create a Strong, Supportive Network

You don't have to—and you shouldn't—go through the recession on your own. Even in good times, freelancers need a network of positive people—other freelancers, friends, and family—who will provide support.

Having freelance friends is especially important. Sharing what you're going through, and knowing that other freelancers are going through the same or similar things, will make you feel better. Other freelancers can also provide advice about what's working for them, and sometimes referrals to clients.

Build the Marketing Habit

Good habits make it easier for you to do things that will help you reach your long-term goals. They also help you focus on what's most important—like marketing your freelance business.

Building a habit actually rewires your brain. So if you build the marketing habit, marketing will be easier for you. Step 3 will show you how to build the marketing habit.

BONUS CONTENT
The Superhero Power You Need to Know About: Grit
How to Boost Your Resilience When Things Go Wrong
Get all bonus content:
www.themightymarketer.com/bonus-fearless-freelancer

Keep Calm and Carry On

In a normal recession, a growth mindset, grit, resilience, and the right actions are enough to thrive. This time, we're also facing way more stress and anxiety due to the pandemic. Our lives will be different. But no one knows what the new normal will look like or how long it will last.

Fortunately, there are many ways, including some quick and easy ways, to manage stress and keep anxiety at bay. Here are a few.

Accept Uncertainty

Freelancing is going to be different, at least for a while. Uncertainty is the new normal. The sooner you accept this, the better off you'll be.

Use a Mantra

Stay calm by using a mantra. Studies show that a mantra—a word, group of words, or a sound—is calming and makes it easier to cope with unexpected stress.

"Keep calm and carry on" is a fitting mantra for the COVID-19 recession. This British slogan became popular in the U.S. during the Great Recession of 2007-2009. When you're feeling stressed, take a deep breath and chant, whisper, or silently say, "I'm going to keep calm and carry on." You'll feel calmer in seconds. Or choose another mantra.

Meditate and/or Practice Yoga

Many studies show that meditation and yoga decrease stress and relieve anxiety. Just 10 minutes a day of meditation and/or an hour a week of practicing yoga will help you feel better. There are lots of great free or low-cost apps and web-based resources that make it easy for you to meditate and/or practice yoga.

Get Outdoors and Exercise

Recent studies show that being in nature helps reduce stress and anxiety. Walking and other physical activity (outdoors or indoors) provide the same benefits while also keeping our bodies strong and healthy.

BONUS CONTENT

11 Ways to Keep Anxiety at Bay and Focus on Freelancing

Get all bonus content:
www.themightymarketer.com/bonus-fearless-freelancer

Key Takeaways

Here's a quick summary of the key takeaways from Step 1:

- Changing what you think will change what happens to your freelance business in a recession.

- Fearless freelancers can thrive despite the recession. You can become a fearless freelancer.

- Every action you take is a small win. And each small win builds your confidence and motivates you to keep taking action.

- Staying calm makes it easier to focus on your freelance business. Ways to stay calm include mantras, meditation, yoga, and exercise.

In Step 2, you'll learn how to stand out in a sea of freelancers and get steady, high-paying clients.

Step 2. Stand Out in a Sea of Freelancers

"If you are not a brand, you are a commodity."
— Philip Kotler

Thrive by Creating a Brand

Freelancers who have a brand and client-focused marketing messages stand out in a sea of freelancers. With less freelance work and more competition in a recession, standing out is more important than ever. In Step 2, you'll learn how to:

- Create your freelance brand so clients view you as better than other freelancers

- Develop client-focused marketing messages so clients know that you're the right freelancer to hire

- Attract more and better clients with your brand and your client-focused marketing messages.

Attract More and Better Clients

What do freelancers have in common with oranges, coal, and cattle? They're all commodities—services (freelancers) and goods (oranges, coal, and cattle) that are largely interchangeable. To many clients, one freelance writer or editor (or another type of freelancer) seems just as good as another—unless you have a freelance brand and client-focused marketing messages.

Most freelancers don't have brands and client-focused marketing messages. If you do, clients will see you as providing more value and being more professional than other freelancers.

You'll stand out in the sea of freelancers. So you'll be able to attract more—and better—clients. And when clients contact you, they'll already understand what you do and how you can help them. So you'll be able to do less marketing.

What's in a Freelance Brand?

Your freelance brand tells clients what to expect from your services. It helps clients get to know and trust you. Also, it helps clients remember you—and think of you first for freelance work.

It takes time and effort to simplify your marketing messages and develop your freelance brand, but it's well worth it. Your freelance brand is made up of:

- Logo and tagline
- Tone of voice
- Colors
- Business name (or your name and title)
- Client-focused marketing messages.

Logo and Tagline

Your logo and tagline are the main ways you show your brand. A logo is an image, symbol, or other design to identify your services. Logos often have an image, but sometimes they're just text in a nice design. A logo should be easily identifiable and simple.

A tagline—one of your key client-focused marketing messages—is a memorable phrase or sentence that helps your target markets understand what you do. Target markets are groups of clients (usually part of an industry) that you work with or want to work with.

Make your tagline short enough to look good with your logo. And make sure it's clear. Clarity always trumps creativity and cleverness in a tagline (and in all marketing). A professional designer will work with you to create a logo that represents your business.

Tone of Voice

Your brand tone of voice expresses your company's values, personality, and way of thinking. It needs to be appropriate for your target markets. For example, if your clients are conservative, you need a formal, conservative tone of voice. But if your clients are creative, your brand should be bolder and more creative.

Colors

Colors, which are associated with specific characteristics, are important too. For example, blue, black, and red are among the most popular colors in brands. Here's what they mean:

- Blue: Trust. Also dependable and strength. Blue is often used in business brands.
- Red: Excitement. Also bold and youthful.
- Black: Powerful and sleek. Black is often used for luxury products.

Your designer can help you choose the right colors for your brand.

BONUS CONTENT
Case Studies: How 3 Freelancers Created Their Brands
Get all bonus content:
www.themightymarketer.com/bonus-fearless-freelancer

Business Name

Most freelancers use their personal names instead of a business name. Having a good business name will help you stand out even more in a sea of freelancers. But even if you use your own name, if you have a strong brand you'll still stand out.

Your business name doesn't have to be unique—and it probably won't be. It should appeal to your target markets, say what you do, and be clear.

Being clever is optional. If you can think of a clever name that appeals to your target markets, that's great. But being clear is far more important than being clever. Use real words or phrases, and stay away from anything that will confuse clients.

If you don't create a business name, make sure your title clearly says what you do. For example, if I didn't have a business name, my title would be Lori De Milto, freelance medical writer. My busines name is Lori De Milto Writer for Rent LLC.

Develop Your Freelance Brand Statement

Your freelance brand statement will help you think about your logo and create your tagline and other client-focused marketing messages. It needs to clearly and concisely state:

- What you offer: Services
- Who you offer it to: Target markets (types of clients)
- How you're different or better than other freelancers.

Here's the formula for a freelance brand statement:

[MY TARGET MARKETS] can count on me for [KEY SERVICES] delivered with [THINGS THAT MAKE ME DIFFERENT, INCLUDING CORE VALUES AND PERSONALITY TRAITS].

Under services and target markets, focus on the work you like best where there are good opportunities for freelancers, even in a recession, and types of clients that can give you steady, high-paying work, even in a recession. You can still do other types of work and work with other types of clients.

My example:

HOSPITALS/HEALTH SYSTEMS, MEDICAL PRACTICES, DISEASE-FOCUSED HEALTH ORGANIZATIONS, AND OTHER CLIENTS can count on me for TARGETED CONTENT delivered ON TIME, EVERY TIME.

Step 4. Choose Your Moneymaking Specialty has more information on the best opportunities for freelancers in a recession.

BONUS CONTENT
Tool: Freelance Brand Statement Template
Get all bonus content:
www.themightymarketer.com/bonus-fearless-freelancer

Position Yourself as Different or Better

And you don't actually have to be different or better than other freelancers. You just need to position yourself as different and better.

So, for example, my freelance brand focuses on delivering targeted medical content and doing this on time every time. Many successful freelance writers deliver content that's targeted to the audience and meets the client's deadlines. So I'm not unique. But using this in my brand positions me as different and better than other freelancers. This positioning makes me stand out in a sea of freelancers.

In your brand statement, base "things that make me different" on client needs. The key overall client need is for you to make the client's life easier. Other general needs are:

- Meet my deadlines
- Stay on my budget
- Do the project right
- Be flexible
- Be responsive.

If the clients you work with have another general need, you can use that. Choose one or a few client needs as the key need(s) for your brand.

In describing things that make you different, you'll use core values and personality traits that will appeal to your target markets. For example, if you choose "do the project right" as the key need for your brand, core values and personality traits could include accurate, meticulous, and/or trustworthy. The brand template has a list of core values and personality traits.

Create Client-Focused Marketing Messages

When a client looks at your LinkedIn profile or website, you want him/her to immediately think, "Yes, this is the right freelancer for me." You make this happen with client-focused marketing messages.

Your brand statement and your tagline are key parts of your client-focused marketing messages. You'll build on these in your LinkedIn profile and website, especially in the heads and subheads.

Here's how this works. My key marketing messages build on my tagline of "Targeted Medical Content. On time. Every time." My LinkedIn profile headline is: "Freelance Medical Writer | Targeted Content to Attract, Engage, and Motivate Your Audience(s) | On time, Every time." My Home page headline is: "Targeted Medical Content that Attracts, Engages, and Motivates Your Audiences."

My key messages are clever, but yours don't have to be. It's much more important to be clear. If clients don't know what your marketing messages mean, they'll move on to the next freelancer on their list.

If you can come up with clever language that contributes to your client-focused marketing messages, that's great. But don't waste time trying to do this. You can always update your marketing messages later, when you've had more time to think about this.

Think About Your Brand and Messages

Think about your freelance brand and client-focused marketing messages as you go through the rest of this book. When you choose or refine your specialty, work on your prospect list, and draft direct emails (Steps 4, 5, and 6), you'll learn more about the needs of clients in your industry(ies) and target markets. After you read about your LinkedIn profile (Step 7) and freelance website (Step 8), come back and work on your freelance brand and client-focused marketing messages. You'll be using them in your LinkedIn profile and website.

Key Takeaways

Here's a quick summary of the key takeaways from Step 2:

- Standing out in a sea of freelancers is critical in a recession.

- Your freelance brand and client-focused marketing messages will help you stand out and attract more and better clients.

- If you have a brand, you can do less marketing because clients will know more about you.

In Step 3, you'll learn how to make marketing easier by making it a habit. After that, you'll learn the seven general steps to marketing that will help you build a stable, successful freelance business. Every step has information about freelancing in a recession.

Step 3. Build the Marketing Habit

"Success is the product of daily habits."
— James Clear

Thrive with Consistent Marketing

Habits make it easier for us to do the things we need to do—like marketing a freelance business. And in a recession, freelancers who want to thrive must do a lot of marketing a lot of the time. In Step 3, you'll learn how to:

- Make marketing like tying your shoelaces, something that gets easier when you do it more
- Build a marketing habit that will stick
- Practice the marketing habit at the right time of the day
- Break the marketing habit into manageable chunks.

Get Steady, High-Paying Clients

Steady, high-paying clients who need freelancers aren't using freelance jobs sites or content mills like fiverr, Upwork, or Freelancer.com. And they're not going to magically find you.

Instead, you have to go out and find them. And you have to attract them with your marketing.

Avoid Freelance Job Sites and Content Mills

Even during good times, freelance pay on freelance jobs sites and content mills is ridiculously low. Stiff competition from other freelancers means that you waste time applying for work you never get. And if you do get the work, the freelance jobs site or content mill will take a cut.

Upwork, the giant of freelance job sites, has fees ranging from 5%-20%. Giving Upwork 5% of your fee may not sound too bad—but to reach the 5% level, you need to do more than $10,000 worth of business—with each client.

In a recession, more freelancers will be competing for fewer gigs. Pay is likely to go even lower.

Freelancers who build the marketing habit don't have to use freelance jobs sites or content mills—because they know how to find and attract high-paying clients.

Make Marketing Easier

A habit is "the small decisions you make and actions you perform every day," says James Clear, best-selling author of *Atomic Habits: An Easy & Proven Way to Build Good Habits & Break Bad Ones. Good Morning America* called Clear the "world's leading expert on habit formation."

The more you practice a habit—in this case the marketing habit—the easier it gets. It's like learning how to tie your shoelaces. In the beginning, you had to really think about what you were doing. And it was hard. But the more times you tied your shoelaces, the easier it got—because tying your shoelaces became a habit.

This book tells you everything you need to know about marketing your freelance business. Use your growth mindset to follow the steps and do the work to make marketing a habit.

Start by Making Time for Marketing

Many freelancers say that they don't have time for marketing. What this really means is that marketing isn't a big enough priority for them.

If you want to thrive in the recession, you must make marketing a top priority. The only professional thing that's more important is always doing great work for your clients.

If your freelance work is slow because of the recession, spend most of your time on marketing. If you're still busy, this could change at any time during a recession. So you still need to make time for marketing.

How to Build Habits that Stick

Here are some simple ways to build the marketing habit, based on the work of Clear, best-selling author Daniel H. Pink, and me.

Use Implementation Intentions

An implementation intention is basically a plan to practice a habit regularly. Here's the formula: I will [BEHAVIOR] at [TIME].

Hundreds of studies have shown that implementation intentions help people stick to their goals. Here's an example of an implementation intention to build the marketing habit: I will WORK ON MY MARKETING at 1 PM ON FRIDAY.

Habit stacking is an implementation intention where after you do something that you already do regularly (a current habit), you practice the new habit. Here's the formula: After [CURRENT HABIT], I will [NEW HABIT]. Here's an example of habit stacking to build the marketing habit: After I CHECK MY EMAIL, I will GO ON LINKEDIN AND LOOK FOR POSTS TO COMMENT ON.

Choose the Right Time of Day

When you do your marketing makes a big difference. In *When? The Scientific Secrets of Perfect Timing*, Daniel Pink divides the day into three parts: peak, trough, and rebound. They occur in this order for most people. Night owls tend to rebound, trough, and peak.

Most of us are at our best during the morning, especially the late morning. Work on things that take the most effort, like starting to draft your client-focused marketing messages (Step 2) during the peak.

In the afternoon, we have less energy and are less alert. This is a good time for easier work like developing your prospect list (Step 5) or searching for relevant contacts to invite to be part of your network on LinkedIn (Step 9).

During the rebound, late afternoon and early evening, we're most creative. Work on things like writing your LinkedIn profile and website content and drafting direct emails then. This is also a good time to refine your marketing messages.

Figure out the science of your day and use it to make building the marketing habit easier.

Start Small and Increase Gradually

Start building the marketing habit with small actions. For example, invite one person to connect with you on LinkedIn each day for the first week. The next week, invite two people to join your network each day. Every action you take helps you build the marketing habit.

Focus on Actions, Not Outcomes

You can't control outcomes, like whether a client hires you. But you have total control over your actions. For example, if you aim to get 3 new clients in 30 days, you're going to be disappointed. Clients rarely need freelancers when we first market to them. And they're less likely to need freelancers soon during a recession.

But you can easily develop a list of 25 prospective clients and send them direct emails over the next 30 days. And actions like this, repeated often, are very likely to result in new clients in the future.

Chunk the Marketing Habit

Break the marketing habit into manageable chunks. Instead of trying to write or revise your LinkedIn profile in one day, for example, try this:

- Day 1: Draft your About section.
- Day 2: Review and refine your About section.
- Day 3: Finalize your About section. Start drafting your headline.
- Day 4: Review and refine your headline.
- Day 5: Work on your Experience section.
- Day 6: Work on the rest of your profile.
- Day 7: Finalize your headline.
- Day 8: Review everything carefully.

This makes it easy to practice the marketing habit consistently and get stuff done.

When You Slip, Get Back on Track

We all slip and get off track. Be kind to yourself and accept that you're human. Then get back to practicing your marketing.

Be Patient

It takes time and practice to build the marketing habit. Keep going and you'll see the results.

BONUS CONTENT

The Habit that Will Make You a Success—Even in a Recession

Tool: The Ultimate Guide to Goals for Freelance Success

Get all bonus content:
www.themightymarketer.com/bonus-fearless-freelancer

Key Takeaways

Here's a quick summary of the key takeaways from Step 3:

- Steady, high-paying clients aren't going to magically find you. You have to do a lot of marketing to find and attract them.

- Freelancers who build the marketing habit can find and attract steady, high-paying clients—even in a recession.

- Like any habit, the more marketing you do, the easier it will be.

- The only thing more important in a recession than marketing is always doing great work for your clients.

In Step 4, you'll learn how to choose a moneymaking specialty(ies). After that, you'll learn how to find steady, high-paying clients within your specialty(ies).

Step 4. Choose Your Moneymaking Specialty(ies)

"If you aim at nothing, you'll hit it every time."
— Zig Ziglar

Thrive by Specializing

Specializing is the fastest, easiest way to get steady, high-paying clients in good times and in bad. In a recession, freelancers with in-demand specialties will stand out in a sea of freelancers. In Step 4, you'll learn how to:

- Make more money by specializing
- Choose or refine your specialty(ies) to thrive in the recession
- Find industries that win and avoid industries that lose in a recession
- Focus on in-demand services.

Make More Money with Less Effort

If you have a bad leak and water is pouring onto your floor, you're going to call a plumber, not a handyman. The plumber is an expert in solving your problem. The handyman isn't.

When clients hire a freelancer, they want an expert too. And they're willing to pay well for that expertise. So you don't have to take whatever work comes along.

Specializing also helps you get the clients you deserve with less work and in less time. By specializing, you'll learn more about your clients (your target markets). You'll know who your prospective clients (prospects) are, where to find them, what they need, and how you can meet those needs. You'll be able to show clients that you understand their needs and have the expertise to help them.

Stand Out in a Sea of Freelancers

Having the right specialty(ies) is even more important when you're freelancing in a recession. As a specialist, you'll stand out in a sea of freelancers. And steady, high-paying clients will be able to find you more easily. Colleagues, a key source of referrals, will also be more likely to remember what you do. Also, as a specialist, you'll build expertise and will be able to work faster and with less effort.

Choose the Right Specialty(ies)

Choosing a specialty, or niche, and moving toward it takes time for most freelancers. Your specialty(ies) can—and usually should—change as you get more experience and learn more about the market for your services. Start more broadly and narrow down your specialty over time.

You can start with two or three specialties, and may even keep two or three specialties throughout your freelance career. In a recession, it's great to have two or three specialties. If one of your specialties takes a nosedive, you still have other clients and freelance work in other specialties.

Decide How to Specialize

A moneymaking specialty offers lots of opportunities for freelancers like you, even in a recession, and makes it easy for you to find and reach prospective clients.

Finding your moneymaking specialty(ies) does take time and effort, but the work you put in now will help you get great clients throughout your freelance career.

Ways to Specialize

The most common ways to specialize are by industry, by project, or by a combination of industry and project. For most freelancers, industry specialization is best, especially if you're fairly new to freelancing or have been freelancing for a while but aren't as successful as you'd like to be. Industry specialization is a broader way to specialize. And it lets you choose industries with lots of opportunities and high-paying clients, even in a recession.

You can do work outside your specialty(ies) too. Clients may ask you to do other types of work for them. Whether you say yes is up to you, but doing work outside your specialty(ies) is a great way to get new experience and possibly expand your specialty(ies). If you do say yes, make sure you can do a great job for the client.

Industry Specialization

Industry specialization means focusing on an industry, part of an industry, and/or target markets (types of client) within an industry.

Example based on my specialty:

- Industry specialty: Medical/healthcare
- Parts of the industry where I focus: Healthcare services and consumer/patient education
- Target markets: Hospitals/health systems, large medical practices, disease-focused health organizations, healthcare communications agencies, and patient education organizations.

Project Specialization

Project specialization is based on services. This is very broad, so it's harder to figure out what type of clients to target. For most freelancers, project specialization is the worst choice during a recession. Examples are writing white papers and case studies, editing books, or web design.

Combined Industry and Project Specialization

The narrowest specialization combines industry and project specialization. Examples are editing for authors of books and web design for the financial services industry.

Combined industry and project specialization let you focus on specific types of clients and services. There's less competition because your specialization is so narrow. This type of specialty generally works best if you're an experienced freelancer and you know your target markets really well.

But unless you're already working in a recession-proof industry(ies) and providing services that are still in high demand, this narrow focus will limit your opportunities.

Go for the Money

Whatever type of specialty(ies) you choose, go for the money. Focus on industries, target markets, specific clients, and projects (services) that offer high pay and lots of opportunities—even in a recession.

The best clients are usually large businesses, especially businesses that sell products or services to other businesses (B2B) rather than to consumers (B2C). There are other types of high-paying clients too (see Step 5).

During the COVID-19 recession, some industries will grow and others will shrink. Some industries could go either way. After studying what experts in investments and innovation are saying, and reading advice from other experts who work with freelancers, here are the likely winners and losers during this recession.

Winning Industries

- DIY home improvement
- E-commerce, including for health products
- E-learning, including homeschooling
- Finance
- Healthcare
- Insurance
- Logistics and delivery
- Pharmaceuticals
- Self-help
- Taxes
- Technology, including for remote work
- Tele-health

Within industries, some parts of the industry or target markets will do better than others. For example, healthcare is usually recession proof. But the COVID-19 recession is different. The coronavirus pandemic put an unheard-of level of stress on hospitals/health systems. They were operating in a crisis mode for months, caring only for patients with COVID-19 and other patients with life-threatening illnesses or injuries.

States mandated that hospitals/health systems couldn't do elective surgery or provide many other services. This sharply reduced revenues. A focus on crisis communications combined with lower revenues led to these clients stopping many projects involving freelancers. Outside of primary care, states essentially shut down most other medical practices. These practices also saw steep reductions in revenue. It will take time for hospitals/health systems and medical practices to get back to business as usual.

But tele-health emerged as a big winner in the COVID-19 recession. Other companies that come up with ways to improve healthcare virtually will also be big winners.

Losing Industries

If you're working in any of these industries, start expanding or change your specialty(ies) now:

- Airlines
- Cruise companies
- Investment banking
- Tourism in general
- Traditional retail
- Oil and gas
- Professional sports and entertainment.

Other Industries

If your industries aren't on the list of winners or losers, they could go either way in the COVID-19 recession. Consider your options and start expanding to some winning industries soon.

In-Demand Services

Along with choosing industries or target markets with high demand, focus on core services that clients still need and are willing to pay for. Content marketing, for example, continues to boom, while writing (or editing) for magazines and newspapers continues to plummet.

The Content Marketing Institute defines content marketing as "a strategic marketing approach focused on creating and distributing valuable, relevant, and consistent content to attract and retain a clearly defined audience—and, ultimately, to drive profitable customer action."

Content marketing focuses on providing relevant and useful content that helps customers and clients solve problems, rather than selling products or services. Most B2B marketers (and many B2C marketers) now use content marketing. The *B2B Content Marketing 2020* report found that half of marketers outsource at least one content marketing activity. Of marketers who outsource, 84% hire freelancers to write content for them. The Content Marketing Institute, MarketingProfs, and Sitecore wrote the report, based on a survey of 1,798 marketers representing many industries, functional areas, and company sizes.

So content marketing is a great core service for freelance writers and also for freelance editors. Businesses that have at least 50 employees are likely to need help with content marketing and be able to pay a freelance writer or editor well.

Other core services include other types of web-based content and any service that helps clients sell their core products and services. Many clients are eliminating or doing fewer print projects now. Printing and mailing a newsletter, for example, costs a lot more than doing e-newsletters. So e-newsletters and web content are core services.

Even clients who are cutting costs still need to market their core services and products. Figure out the core services within specific industries or target markets, and even for individual clients. Then focus on services you already provide or could provide that match client needs.

Assess Your Industries, Target Markets, and Services

Take what's happening in the economy and apply it to your freelance business. Ask yourself four questions:

1. What was going right before the COVID-19 pandemic?

2. What has already changed?
3. What do I expect to change over the next six months or so?
4. What do I need to do to thrive despite the recession?

If you're a new freelancer, make your best guesses about what you think would have happened in the first two years of your business if the pandemic did not happen.

BONUS CONTENT
Tool: Simple Strategic Plan for Surviving the Recession
Get all bonus content:
www.themightymarketer.com/bonus-fearless-freelancer

Look for target markets within your industry(ies) that are growing or at least staying about the same or not declining much. Also look for target markets with professional associations where you can learn about freelance work, find and reach clients, and network. Look for services where demand is still high.

Industry Analysis

Use Dun & Bradstreet to learn more about the industry(ies) that you're working in or want to work in. Select each industry you want to assess and click on Industry Analysis.

I didn't see any dates on the industry analysis, so these may not have been updated since the COVID-19 recession started. Form a full picture of each industry by combining what you learn on Dun & Bradstreet with the information above and what you learn from networking with other freelancers and from your professional associations. Dun & Bradstreet is also a great tool for finding prospects (see Step 5).

Networking

Networking with other freelancers online and in person is the best way to assess target markets and learn which services clients need most. Meet other freelancers in professional associations and in groups and forums for freelancers, like:

- Online forums of professional associations
- LinkedIn
- Freelance Success, an online community of professional, nonfiction writers.

You can find other freelancers at meetings and conferences of professional associations and through membership directories or member lists of online communities and professional associations. Ask them about their experiences with the target markets you're working in or considering.

Learn more about how to build your network in a way that feels comfortable, not scary, in Step 9.

Professional Associations

Professional associations are vital to a successful freelance business for many reasons. In choosing your specialty(ies), professional associations help you learn about target markets and stay updated on what's happening, and find clients to market to through their member directories. You can also build a strong network through professional associations, which will help you get more referrals (also covered under Step 9).

Before joining a professional association, check out the website and available resources, and try to go to a meeting or conference. The American Medical Writers Association has played a key role in my success. I've been a member since the year after I started my business. I've joined several other associations over the years but none have been nearly as helpful to me in terms of networking and learning.

Make Your Choices

Build your business faster and with less effort by starting with what you know. Use your experience from freelancing and jobs, and if you're a recent college graduate, what you learned getting your degree. You can change or expand your specialty(ies) later.

Choose the clients you want to work with (your industries and target markets) and the services you provide. Focus first on the industries and types of clients and where you have the most chance of success because of your background, experience, and skills. For example, if you worked full time as a writer for a Fortune 500 company, focus on large businesses. If you were a graphic designer for a university, focus on colleges and universities. And if you don't have much or any work experience, focus on something related to your college degree or other training.

Prioritize your industries, target markets, and services based on client needs in a recession, your experience, your expertise, and your interests. If you're a new freelancer or you're working in industries that have shrunk or been destroyed by the recession, you still want to focus on industries, target markets, and specific clients that offer high pay and lots of opportunities now. But you'll probably have to work with the smaller clients in these industries and target markets for a while.

These clients will pay less than bigger clients. But that's okay—because your goal as a new freelancer or a freelancer moving into new industries is to get experience. You'll use that experience to move on to bigger clients who can pay you more.

BONUS CONTENT
Want to Worry Less and Make More Money? Be a Specialist
Get all bonus content:
www.themightymarketer.com/bonus-fearless-freelancer

Describe Your Specialty(ies)

Draft a specialty description using this formula:

I help [WHO YOU HELP] do [WHAT THEY WANT TO ACHIEVE] so [WHY THEY CARE ABOUT ACHIEVING IT].

Here's my example:

I help hospitals/health systems, medical practices, disease-focused health organizations, and other clients engage, inform, and motivate target audiences so hospitals/health systems and medical practices can grow their businesses and disease-focused health organizations and patient education organizations can help more people stay healthy or live better.

It's okay if you don't know enough to do this yet. And your specialty description doesn't have to be perfect. It's just for you, to help you understand how to target your marketing. You'll probably use some, but not all, of the description in your marketing.

Write as much of your specialty description as you can now. After you finish this book, come back and complete it.

You'll use the description of your specialty and your brand statement (Step 2) to develop marketing that will help you attract steady, high-paying clients.

Key Takeaways

Here's a quick summary of the key takeaways from Step 4:

- Specializing is always the fastest, easiest way to get steady, high-paying clients. In a recession, having a moneymaking specialty(ies) is even more important.

- A moneymaking specialty(ies) offers lots of opportunities for freelancers like you even in a recession and makes it easy for you to find and reach prospective clients.

- Focus on industries and target markets where demand is high even in a recession and clients can still afford to pay you well. Also, focus on core services that clients still need.

- To find the best specialty(ies), consider what's happening in the economy and what's happening in your freelance business. Do research and network to learn which industries, target markets, and clients will be best for you.

- Choosing and defining your specialty(ies) takes time. It's okay to have two or three specialties. And your specialty(ies) can—and usually should—change over time.

In Step 5, you'll learn how to find great prospective clients within your specialty(ies). After that, you'll learn how to reach and attract them with your marketing, including direct email.

Step 5. Find the Right Prospects

"Opportunities are usually disguised as hard work,
so most people don't recognize them."
— Ann Landers

Thrive by Choosing Your Clients

Having a clearly defined specialty(ies) makes it much easier to find steady, high-paying clients in a recession. In Step 5, you'll learn how to:

- Choose the high-paying clients you want to work with (your prospects)
- Find the right people to target within each organization (your contacts)
- Get the hard-to-find information you need to reach your contacts.

You'll learn how to use professional associations to quickly and easily develop your prospect lists and how to prioritize your prospects to get steady, high-paying clients faster.

Make Your Prospect Lists

Develop prospect lists of about 200-400 companies and other organizations you'd like to work with. Do a separate list for each target market. Choose about 30-40 prospects for now so you learn the process, and add more later.

Let's start with the right type of prospects to look for: Prospects most likely to hire you and steady, high-paying clients. Then we'll cover how to find them and the information you need about each prospect.

Choose the Prospects Most Likely to Hire You

Choose clients in the industry(ies) you identified in your specialty. Here's how this works, using my specialty as an example. My general specialty is "Freelance medical writer for healthcare marketers and health organizations." That's somewhat broad, so I need to pick certain target markets to focus on. My specialty description includes specific target markets: hospitals/health systems, medical practices, disease-focused health organizations, and other clients.

Hospitals and disease-focused health organizations are easy to find, so I focused my prospect lists on these. "Other clients" is a broad term that includes organizations that I hear about and add to my prospect list and other clients that find me.

In making your list, focus first on the prospects that are most likely to hire you based on your background, experience, and skills. New freelancers, for example, aren't likely to land Apple or Mayo Clinic as clients. When I started out, I focused on smaller hospitals. As I gained more experience, I began to target—and get—larger, more prestigious hospitals, like Johns Hopkins Medicine. Expand your prospect list to other clients as you gain experience.

Go for the Money

Also focus on clients that are likely to pay freelancers well and have steady work for us. You can't be sure that a client is high-paying and uses freelancers regularly unless you know another freelancer who works for them. But my proven freelance marketing process helps you find and market to the companies and other organizations that are most likely to be steady, high-paying clients.

The best clients are usually large businesses, especially businesses that that sell products or services to other businesses (B2B) rather than to consumers (B2C). In general, large businesses make the best clients because they often work with multiple freelancers, understand the value we bring them, and can pay us what we're worth.

But there are other types of high-paying clients too, such as some foundations, some non-profit organizations, and some universities. Some smaller companies are great clients too. The word "company" in this book refers to any type of organization that hires freelancers.

Find high-paying clients for your prospect list through:
- Professional associations
- Dun & Bradstreet
- Leading company lists (e.g., Inc. 5000 and Fortune 500)
- Online industry directories (e.g., Medical Marketing & Media top 100 agencies)
- LinkedIn.

Do It the Easy Way

Using the member directories of professional associations is the easiest way to develop prospect lists. Member directories have all or most of the information you need, including a good contact person for each company and, usually, his/her email address.

If you're new to freelancing or still figuring out where to focus, professional associations will help you find prospects you might not have thought to look for on your own. General business associations like the American Marketing Association and the International Association of Business Communicators can be especially useful if you're still defining your specialty(ies) or exploring different specialties.

Joining one or a few professional associations is a lot cheaper than the cost of the time it will take you to develop your prospect list using other research. If you don't already belong to professional associations in your target markets, join now.

But there are many steady, high-paying clients that don't belong to professional associations. So use other sources too.

Dun & Bradstreet

Dun & Bradstreet is a great tool for finding high-quality business prospects. To be listed on Dun & Bradstreet, companies need a D-U-N-S number (data universal numbering system). These numbers basically mean that the company is reliable and stable.

Dun & Bradstreet lets you look up companies by industry and then by sectors (target markets) within each industry. The search results give you the list of companies with their sales revenue. You can also search by number of employees. When you click on a company, you get its profile.

The number of results you can get for free is limited. But it's an easy way to find some high-quality prospects. Make sure you search by your country/region.

Use LinkedIn (covered below) to find the right contact person (people).

Leading Company Lists and Online Directories

Leading company lists and online directories in your industries are also great ways to find companies you want to work with. Then, use LinkedIn to find the right contact person (people).

Leading company lists like Inc. 5000 and Fortune 500 list the top companies in general or in a target market (e.g., best hospitals in the U.S.). Like the companies listed in Dun & Bradstreet, these are likely to be high-paying clients who can give freelancers steady work.

Inc. 5000 lists the 5,000 fastest-growing privately-held companies in the U.S., with revenue and growth. You can search by industry, but there are only six industry choices.

Fortune 500 companies are big companies. Together, they represent two-thirds of the U.S. gross domestic product. You can also search this list by industry. There are dozens of industries to choose from.

For newer freelancers, Inc. 5000 is a better source of prospects unless you have a very strong track record in your industry(ies) from other work experience. Fortune 500 companies are most likely to hire experienced freelancers.

Use leading company lists to find companies you want to work with. Then use LinkedIn to find the right contact person (people).

Online industry directories list companies in a specific industry. For example, for my hospital prospect list, I used U.S. News & World Report's list of top hospitals and top children's hospitals. In the past, I've used the National Cancer Institute's list of cancer centers to develop a list of cancer centers. I know about these lists because I know my target markets.

Find the right directories for your specialty through a Google search, your professional associations, and networking.

LinkedIn

LinkedIn was more helpful for general prospect searches before Microsoft acquired it in 2016 and did away with the advanced search feature. This change limits what you can do with a free account, and it limits the number of searches you can do each month.

With a free account, LinkedIn is best for finding contacts in the companies you know you want to work with and for finding related prospects through People Also Viewed. The regular search engine is pretty good in helping you find people since LinkedIn's algorithm sorts results by relevance. Even if you get a lot of search results, the top ones should be relevant.

Search results are also based on your connections, so the larger your network, the more results you'll get. This is another reason to have a large, relevant LinkedIn network (at least 500 relevant connections), along with appearing higher in search results when clients are looking for a freelancer. Relevant connections are people in your industry(ies) and target markets and other freelancers. (The details below are based on LinkedIn's Search feature and policies as of August 2020.)

To find the right contact person (people), click the Search bar, click People, and then click All filters. Now you can search by your connections, industry, current company, location (e.g., the United States), and language. If you know a company (or companies) you want to work with, search for that company, and then use Keywords to find people with the right job titles (covered below).

When you find someone who is a good prospect for you, check out his/her People Also Viewed section. This is a great way to find colleagues at the same company who may be better prospects for you and people at different, but similar, companies with the same/similar job title. Members choose whether to show People Also Viewed, so you may not find this for everyone.

With a free account, you can search for 1st- and 2nd-degree connections, but LinkedIn only lets you search for so many people each month. They call this the Commercial Use Limit, but they don't say what the limit is. So do your most important searches first, and know that you can do more searches after the first of the next month.

If you need or want to find a lot of prospects fast, try a premium subscription. You can buy this for a few months, develop your prospect lists, and then go back to the free account.

There are two plans that are good for freelancers: Premium Business or Sales Navigator. Premium Business is $47.99 a month if you get an annual plan and a little more if you pay each month. Sales Navigator starts at $79.99 a month.

Both types of premium accounts give you unlimited browsing up to 3rd-degree connections. The only real benefit of Sales Navigator over Premium Business is that Sales Navigator gives you an advanced search function. So you can search by function, seniority, and more. This makes prospect searches a little faster. I have a Premium Business account and think this works great for freelancers.

Find the Right Contact Person (People)

Look for the types of people who usually hire freelancers or manage the people who hire freelancers. These are usually vice presidents, managers, directors, associate directors, and editors. The right contact person usually works in departments like communications, content marketing, digital marketing, marketing, new business development, sales, or web content. The titles and departments vary in different companies and different target markets. As you learn more about your target markets, you'll learn the best search terms.

Finding the right contact person or people isn't always easy. But if you get close to the right person, and send a professional, client-focused direct email (Step 6), people will forward your message to their colleagues. This has happened to me—and led to new clients—lots of times.

It's good to have several names from each company because sometimes it's difficult to find the right person. Having several contacts is especially helpful for larger companies where multiple departments may use freelancers or you're not sure which person hires freelancers.

Find Email Addresses

Email addresses are difficult to find unless you're using a professional association member directory. These directories usually have email addresses for members.

On LinkedIn, many contacts at client companies don't include their email address under contact info. Don't try to market to them through LinkedIn messages. Most clients don't like this and won't respond. And many clients are rarely on LinkedIn and won't even see your message until long after you've sent it.

I've found a trick for finding email addresses that usually works. Find the format for email addresses on the company's website and then apply it to your contact's name. Try the Newsroom, which always lists media contacts, usually by name and with an actual email address.

I've nearly always been able to find email addresses either in member directories or on the company's website. The few times I haven't been able to find an email address, I've just moved on to the next prospect on my list.

But there are other ways to find email addresses. These include Hunter.io, an extension for Google Chrome and the ZoomInfo plugin to Outlook.

Organize and Prioritize Your Prospect Lists

Put your prospect lists for each target market into a spreadsheet, database, or even a Word file; whatever works for you is fine. For each client, include: Company name, name of contact person, title, department, and email address. For each contact person, include the name, title, department, and email address. Now divide each prospect list into three categories:

- **Hot Prospects**: Companies you most want to work with
- **Routine Prospects**: Companies you'd like to work with
- **Lukewarm Prospects**: Companies you don't really want to work with but will for now to get some experience, make some money, etc.

Where you focus most of your marketing usually depends on the stage of your freelance business. If you're a new freelancer, focus mostly on lukewarm and routine prospects, which are easier to get. If you're an experienced freelancer who wants to be a lot more successful, focus mostly on lukewarm and routine prospects, which are easier to get. And if you're a seasoned, successful freelancer looking for a "tune-up" (new opportunities and/or better clients), focus mostly on hot prospects. But in a recession, freelancers at all stages may need to work with some companies that they wouldn't want to work with in normal times.

BONUS CONTENT
Tool: Prospect List Template
Get all bonus content:
www.themightymarketer.com/bonus-fearless-freelancer

Become an Expert

Making a prospect list also helps you learn more about your target markets and specific clients. This will help you develop the client-focused marketing that attracts steady, high-paying clients.

As you work on your lists and visit prospects' websites, make notes about the challenges they face, the language they use, and their values. Pick a few companies on your prospect list that you'd really like to work with and spend some extra time visiting their websites and taking notes.

Doing this type of research will help you begin to understand what's important to clients in your target market and what they need most. This will help you figure out what to say when you reach out to them to get their attention and show that you can meet their needs.

When I developed my list of hospitals, for example, I found that I had to use different language to appeal to regular hospitals and children's hospitals. All hospitals have the same basic need: to get more business, which means attracting more patients. But my marketing for regular hospitals focused on the business need of attracting more patients, while my marketing for children's hospitals was softer and focused on helping them give more sick kids the best care available. I learned about the need for a different approach with children's hospitals through my research.

Key Takeaways

Here's a quick summary of the key takeaways from Step 5:

- Choose prospects in your specialty(ies) that are most likely to have steady, high-paying work for freelancers even in a recession. These are mostly large businesses, which usually work with multiple freelancers and can pay us what we're worth.

- Focus on clients that are most likely to hire you based on your background, experience, and skills. Expand your list to other clients later.

- Professional associations, through their member directories, are the easiest way to develop prospect lists of steady, high-paying clients. You can also find prospects through Dun & Bradstreet, leading company lists, online directories, and LinkedIn.

- Making prospect lists helps you attract steady, high-paying clients because you become an expert who understands their needs.

In Step 6, you'll use your specialty(ies) and your prospect lists to reach and attract the right clients.

Step 6. Reach and Attract the Right Clients with Direct Email

*"The truth is that nobody cares about you—
they care about what you can do for them."*
— Melonie Dodaro

Thrive by Being Direct

When done right, direct email is very effective in attracting steady, high-paying clients. By carefully targeting clients who can pay you what you're worth and focusing your direct email on their needs, you make yourself irresistible to them. In Step 6, you'll learn how to:

- Use what you've learned working on your specialty and prospect lists to show you understand client needs
- Write direct emails that clients will read
- Start to build relationships with prospects and turn them into clients.

Why You Must Use Direct Email

Choosing the clients you want to work with (by building your prospect lists) and then reaching out to them through direct email gives you control over your freelance work. Direct email frees you from low-paying, high-competition freelance jobs sites and content mills. It frees you from taking whatever work comes along—usually for low-paying clients who don't treat you right.

Stand Out from Other Freelancers

Most freelancers don't use direct email. They don't know about it or think it's email marketing. It's not. Email marketing—what annoys most of us—makes the same offer to thousands of people. The email may use your name, but it's not customized to your needs. Often, email marketing isn't even relevant.

Instead, each direct email is carefully customized to the client and focused on what you can do for that client. If you use direct email—and do it right—you'll stand out. And you'll attract the attention of steady, high-paying clients.

Send your direct email to one contact person at a time if you have more than one contact person for a client. If that person hasn't responded about a month after you sent the follow-up email (covered below), try the next person on your list.

Make More Money

As you read the rest of this chapter, you'll probably think that direct email is a lot of work. That's true.

But here's the thing. You only need a few steady, high-paying clients to make more money and begin to build a stable, successful freelance business.

And think about the value of each new client over the next 1, 2, 5, or 10 years. The amount of money you'll make in, say, two years from a new client is well worth the time you spend on direct email.

Attract Clients by Focusing on Their Needs

In Steps 2 and 4, you began to learn about the needs of clients in your target markets. Now we're going to cover the four types of client needs:

- General
- Freelancer-specific
- Target-market or industry
- Company-specific.

By focusing your marketing on a few key needs of clients in your target markets, you'll make yourself irresistible to them. Common general client needs are:

- Get more business or make more money (usually by selling more products or services)
- Help their clients get more business
- Be seen as a thought leader
- Educate and inform people
- Stay on budget and on deadline.

If you focus on getting more business or making more money, you need to break this down into the way the target market does this.

Here are some examples of general needs for different target markets. Hospitals (one of my target markets) need to get more patients in a competitive marketplace (get more business). Communications agencies need to help their clients get more business, make more money, and stay on budget and on deadline. Non-profit organizations need to educate and inform people, get more funding (this is the non-profit version of making more money), and stay on budget.

Freelancer-specific needs start with working with freelancers who are excellent at what they do (writing, editing, etc.). Clients also need:

- Experience in the type of work they're looking for help with (usually)
- Ability to meet deadlines (the key to repeat business)
- Excellent communication skills
- Flexibility, accessibility, and responsiveness
- Ability to take ownership of the project.

Target-market needs and industry-specific needs take more time to learn about. Professional associations are an easy way to do this. They offer great resources and give you opportunities to network with people in your target markets and other freelancers working with clients in your target markets.

Also, follow industry news. There's lots of great free information on the web. Easy ways to learn and stay updated include Google alerts, email newsletters like Smart Briefs, and online publications and websites in your industries and target markets.

Sometimes you can use the same industry need in all direct emails to a specific type of client, with a little customization to the specific client. For example, all hospitals need to get more business (patients) but face intense competition from other hospitals. I use this basic need in all of my direct emails to hospitals, and customize the language I use for each hospital based on its website.

Learn about the needs of each company by spending a few minutes on the prospect's website. The Home and About pages usually have all of the information you need. Make notes about the prospect's mission/vision/values and needs, and the key language used.

Which Needs Should You Focus on?

You only need to focus on a few needs in your direct emails and other marketing. Choose what's most important to the target market, and always include target-market or company-specific needs.

Attract Clients with Compelling Copy

Write a short, targeted direct email to each prospect that combines your knowledge of the target market or industry with some of the language or concepts used on the prospect's website.

Writing the first direct email for each target market does take time. But this will be your template for other clients in that target market. Then you can modify the template for each client in a few minutes. And as you build the marketing habit (Step 3), writing direct emails will become easier for you.

Include the Key Content

Compelling direct email copy:

- Has a client-focused subject line
- Focuses on a key client need and how you meet that need
- Includes brief, relevant experience/background
- Includes a call to action
- Includes your contact information.

BONUS CONTENT

Tool: Direct Email Swipe File, with templates and examples

Get all bonus content:
www.themightymarketer.com/bonus-fearless-freelancer

Write the subject line, the most important part of the email, last. Include the client's name and the organization's name. Focus on client needs and how you meet their needs.

After greeting the contact, show that you understand the company's needs. Then write one or two sentences about how your most relevant experience enables you to meet the client's needs. Include a link to your client-focused website (or your client-focused LinkedIn profile if you don't have a website yet) so that the client can easily learn more about you.

Your call to action should clearly say what will happen next (e.g., "Should we schedule a call next week to discuss this?").

Make it easy for the client to get in touch with you by including an email signature that has your phone number and email address. If you have a logo and tagline, including this in your email signature will help you stand out from other freelancers. Also include your website or LinkedIn profile URL again, too, so the client can easily learn more about you.

Be Compelling

Compelling direct email copy is short, easy to read, personal, and relevant. Keep your direct email short: no more than six sentences. Write short, easy-to-read sentences and paragraphs. Use a subhead for a key client-focused message.

Make each direct email personal by using the contact's name and the company's name. Include the company's name in the subject line and again in the email. Greet the person by name.

Use some of the company's language and/or values in your email. Focus on what the client wants to know about you.

New Freelancers

If you're a new freelancer, focus on whatever relevant experience you have and your abilities. For example, if you're a doctor transitioning into medical writing, highlight the deep knowledge of medicine your clinical experience gives you. If you're a recent college graduate, highlight relevant classes.

Increase Responses by Following Up

Most of your responses won't come from your original email. Instead, they come from your follow-up emails. That's because clients are really busy. They may miss your email or mean to respond to it but don't get to it.

If you don't hear back from a prospect in about a week, follow up. It's super easy to write a follow-up email. You just forward your original email with a short, polite message like:

> "Hi Jane. I thought I'd follow up about my April 21st email (forwarded below) to see if we should connect. I'd love to learn more about ABC Hospital's freelance needs and the ways in which I can help you meet those needs."

How Many Direct Emails Should You Send?

You can't just send out a handful of direct emails and expect to be swamped with freelance work from new clients. If you do direct email right, you can expect a response rate of 2%-5%—in normal times. Here's the math if you develop a list of about 200-400 prospects (as per Step 5):

- 200 direct emails = 4-10 possible clients
- 400 direct emails = 8-20 possible clients.

Marketing in a Recession

But these aren't normal times. In a recession, clients still need freelancers, but many clients cut back on or stop doing marketing projects they normally assign to freelancers.

You can still get steady, high-paying clients during a recession. But you'll need to do more direct emails because your response rate will be lower.

Responses from Interested Clients

And a response doesn't mean that the client wants to hire you right away. That's why I called these possible clients.

Up to 90% of the time, clients don't need a freelancer when you first contact them. Also, it takes time for many clients to decide to hire you.

Once in a while, you might get lucky and reach a client who needs freelance help right away. What usually happens is that the client says they'll keep you in mind for future freelance work or put you in their freelance database. I call these interested clients.

Get More Clients with Continuous Follow-Up

Interested clients are very likely to hire you within the next 12 months or so—if you make sure they think of you first when they need freelance help. You do this by following up with them regularly.

Many freelancers miss out in getting steady, high-paying clients because they never or rarely follow up. Step 10 will show you how to follow up in a way that's comfortable and not pushy.

Get More Clients Sooner

If you really need to get new clients fast, develop a bigger prospect list and send out more direct emails. The more direct emails you send, the more likely it is that you'll hit some clients who need freelance help right away, or at least within a few months.

Plan Your Direct Email Campaigns

Create a separate direct email campaign for each target market. A campaign is a fancy way of saying an organized, strategized effort to achieve a specific goal, in your case, getting steady, high-paying clients.

Start with one target market where you think clients are most likely to hire you based on your current experience. Divide each target market prospect list into groups of about 50 prospects. Each group is a separate direct email campaign.

Send out about 25 direct emails each week. This may sound like a lot, but you need to do a lot of marketing during a recession to get steady, high-paying clients.

Make Direct Email a Habit

As you send more direct emails, doing this will become a habit. Once direct email becomes a habit, it will be easier and you'll do it faster.

Schedule the direct emails on your calendar. You can draft your direct emails at any time that works for you. But send them out on Tuesdays, Wednesdays, or Thursdays when clients are most likely to read them. You can send the direct emails over three days or all on one day; whatever works best for you is fine. Remember to schedule your follow-up emails on your calendar too. Send these out about a week after your original email to all prospects who haven't responded.

Key Takeaways

Here's a quick summary of the key takeaways from Step 6:

- Direct email, when customized to each prospect and focused on client needs, is very effective in getting steady, high-paying clients.
- In a recession, you need to send more direct emails than in good times.
- Effective direct emails have a compelling subject line and are concise, easy to read, and personalized.
- Most responses come from follow-up emails, sent about a week after the original email.
- Get more steady, high-paying clients by continuing to follow up with clients who are interested in your services but don't hire you right away.

Steps 7 and 8 will cover how to develop a strong online presence so that clients who get your direct emails will be impressed when they check you out. Step 7 covers your LinkedIn profile, and Step 8 covers your freelance website.

Step 7. Develop a Client-Focused LinkedIn Profile

"If your LinkedIn profile doesn't showcase your skills and portray you as a polished professional, you are letting the ultimate opportunity just slip away..."
— Donna Serdula

Thrive by Impressing Clients on LinkedIn

Clients expect to be able to check out freelancers before contacting us about freelance work, and colleagues want to know we're professional before they refer work to us. To get steady, high-paying clients in a recession, you must have a strong online presence: your LinkedIn profile and your website. In Step 7, you'll learn how to:

- Develop a client-focused LinkedIn profile
- Write a compelling headline and summary, the keys to attracting steady, high-paying clients
- Use the "magic" words that will help clients find you.

You'll be able to use much or all of the work you put into your LinkedIn profile on your website (covered in Step 8). You can also use this content in professional association member profiles and freelance directories and in online forum bios.

Develop a Complete, Client-Focused Profile

In my 2019 survey of how freelancers market their services, 95% of freelancers who use social networks for business use LinkedIn. And 61% of the freelancers who use LinkedIn say it's "important" or "very important" in getting clients.

More clients are using LinkedIn to search for freelancers now. They're also going there to check us out if they hear about us through a referral or our marketing. And colleagues want to know that the freelancers they refer to clients have professional profiles.

When LinkedIn generates search results, profile completeness and relevant keywords in the headline are at the top of the search algorithm criteria. Other key criteria are your skills, covered in this step, and criteria covered in Step 9: common connections with the person who's doing the search, connections by degree (1st, 2nd, or 3rd), and your activity.

Complete Your Profile

Only 51% of LinkedIn users have complete profiles. So you'll outrank almost half of all members just by completing your profile. If you have an All-Star rating, your profile is complete. To get an All-Star rating, you need to include the right content and have at least 50 connections. The right content is:
- Industry and location
- Profile photo
- Current position (under Experience)
- Two past positions
- Education
- At least three skills.

Create a Compelling Introduction Card

The top part of your profile is called the introduction card. The introduction card includes your:
- Name
- Headline
- Profile photo
- Banner image
- Current position
- Education
- Location
- Contact info.

Your introduction card is the first thing clients see when they click on your profile. Make sure that your headline is compelling and your photo and banner image are professional and clear.

Use Your Brand and Client-Focused Marketing Messages

Stand out in a sea of freelancers, and persuade clients to choose you instead of another freelancer by using your brand statement and client-focused marketing messages from Step 2.

Here's the formula for your freelance brand statement again:

[MY TARGET MARKETS] can count on me for [KEY SERVICES] delivered with [THINGS THAT MAKE ME DIFFERENT, INCLUDING CORE VALUES AND PERSONALITY TRAITS].

Use this to develop client-focused marketing messages for your LinkedIn profile and your website. In your LinkedIn profile, you'll use these marketing messages in your headline and your About section. Read the rest of this step and Step 8. Then go back to Step 2 and work on your brand statement and marketing messages.

Focus on Your Headline

The most important part of your LinkedIn profile is the headline. You can use up to 120 characters to attract clients and make them want to learn more about you. Clearly say what you do and how you help your clients.

Use relevant keywords to rank higher in search results, especially "freelancer" and "freelance [writer, editor, etc.]" and your services. You can also include the type of clients you work with or other key information. Here are a few examples of dull and compelling client-focused headlines.

Dull

Lori De Milto
President at LDM Company

Compelling

Lori De Milto
Freelance medical writer of targeted content, on time, every time

Dull

Bob Smith
Independent business owner

Compelling

Bob Smith
Freelance writer specializing in helping financial services companies attract and retain customers and clients

Dull
> Jane Jones
> Editor

Compelling
> Jane Jones
> Freelance editor, delivering clear, accurate content to help small businesses succeed

Use a Professional Photo

Experts say that people with profile photos get 14-21 times more profile views than people without photos. And having a professional photo on your LinkedIn profile makes it much more likely that clients will take you seriously. A professional photo shows the client that you're a professional and that you're worth the money they'll pay for your services.

It's best to hire a professional photographer to take your photo, which you can also use on your website and in other marketing. A professional photographer will make you look your best, even if you're like me and hate to be photographed.

If you don't hire a pro, don't use a selfie. Make sure the background for your photo is neutral and clean. Make sure your face is centered and there's a little space over your head. Don't include your pet or kids in your LinkedIn photo. The photo size is 400 x 400 pixels, with a maximum size of 10MB.

Use an Effective Banner Image

The banner image, sometimes called the cover photo, is the bar at the top of your profile that includes your photo. Your photo is on the left in the banner image on computers and centered on smart phones and tablets. The default banner image is fine. If you use a custom image, make sure it's clear and looks great as part of your profile on computers, smart phones, and tablets. The banner image size is 1,584 x 396 pixels, with a maximum size of 4MB.

Include Your Contact Info

Make it easy for clients to contact you by including at least your email address and, if you're comfortable, your phone number in Contact info and again in About. Also include your website in both places. This is basic, but freelancers often forget to do this. To add your contact details, go to the bottom of your introduction card and click on Contact info.

Include Your Industry

Your industry is a key part of LinkedIn's search algorithm. If you want to have a complete profile and rank higher in search results, include your industry. To add your industry, click edit on your introduction card and scroll down to Industry.

Engage Clients in About

The About section is the second most important part of your profile after your headline. And the first 220-270 characters with spaces count most. That's what shows before clients have to click see more. On mobile devices, about 102-167 characters show.

Make sure the first 220-270 characters build on your headline and offer a clear, concise client-focused message. Put as much of your key message as you can in the first 102-167 characters to attract clients viewing your profile on a smart phone or tablet.

Here are a few examples of the beginning of About sections that will bore or drive away clients and what do to instead.

Boring or Worthless

I'm actively seeking clients who need someone to write their medical documents. I work on . . .

Engaging

Count on me for medical content that engages your target audiences. I help healthcare marketers and health organizations effectively communicate with patients, providers, and other audiences. (192 characters)

Boring or Worthless
I own MyLastName Company. I have skills that are rare among freelance writers and am passionate. . . .

Engaging
Irresistible content helps businesses attract more clients and customers. As a freelance copywriter, I write irresistible websites, blogs, and other online content to help you build your business. (196 characters)

Boring or Worthless
I have been working as a freelance editor since November 2014. I enjoy editing . . .

Engaging
As a freelance editor who specializes in working with small businesses, I deliver clear, accurate content that will help you impress your clients and customers—without spending a fortune. (189 characters)

Use the Right Keywords

Continue to use the keywords that clients are likely to use to search for a freelancer like you throughout About. Clients often look for keywords related to titles, so use "freelancer" instead of "freelance services," and "freelance medical writer" (or "freelance ADD YOUR FIELD HERE") instead of "freelance medical writing."

Use other keywords related to your services that people will search for, like the type of clients you work with, your key services, and industry-specific keywords.

Include Just Enough Key Content

Focus the rest of About on how you help your clients meet their needs. Briefly summarize your services and your relevant experience and background. Use bulleted lists for your services and anything else that works well in a list. Include some samples of your freelance work under Media.

Include a Call to Action

A call to action tells clients what you want them to do. The call to action can invite clients to call or email you, visit your website, connect on LinkedIn, or any combination of these. Include a call to action, with your contact information, at the end of About.

Highlight Your Experience

This is the section for your positions. Your freelance business is your current position. Include "freelance" in your title followed by what you do (e.g., freelance writer or editor).

And you can repeat some of the information from About here. Continue to include relevant keywords.

If you've had professional jobs before becoming a freelancer, list at least two of them here. Include details about your work and achievements. Focus on what's most relevant to your freelance work and your target clients. If the organizations you worked for are impressive, include a brief description of each.

And if you haven't had two other professional jobs, include other relevant work experience here, such as college internships or part-time work. To add/edit experience go to the Experience section. To edit a job, click the edit pencil to the right of the job. To add a new job, click the + on the right of Experience.

Include Education, Skills, and Projects

Your education, which is necessary for a complete profile, helps you highlight your expertise and experience. LinkedIn says you need at least three skills for a complete profile. People with at least 5 skills get 17 times more profile views than people without skills, say some experts. And listing skills is another way to rank higher in search results. To add/edit skills, scroll down to Skills & Endorsements then click on Add a new skill.

Adding relevant projects that you've worked on lets you highlight your skills and experience and helps you rank higher in search results. You can include projects from school here, which is helpful to recent college graduates. To add/edit projects, go to the Accomplishments section, then click on the + on the right for the dropdown menu, and choose Projects.

Include Other Relevant LinkedIn Profile Sections

Other sections of your profile that are also helpful for freelancers are volunteer experience, accomplishments, and interests. If you volunteer, including for professional associations, mention your volunteer work. This is especially helpful if you're a recent college graduate with little or no work experience or a new freelancer. To add/edit volunteer experience go to the Accomplishments section. Click on the + on the right for the dropdown menu, then choose Organizations. Describe what you've done as a volunteer under Position Held.

The Accomplishments section is for these accomplishments: Projects, Organizations, Courses, Publications, Certifications, Honors & Awards, Patents, and Test Scores. The two most relevant types of accomplishments on LinkedIn for freelancers are projects, covered earlier, and organizations. Under organizations, add your professional associations and your role in them (e.g., member, committee member, or officer). If you're a recent college graduate or a new freelancer who's taken relevant courses, add some courses too.

If you have other accomplishments that fit these categories, include them. But don't worry if you can't add more information to this section.

To add/edit accomplishments, go to the Accomplishments section of your profile. Click on the + on the right for the dropdown menu, then choose the category you want to add info to.

Interests include the influencers, companies, groups, and schools you follow. This section isn't crucial, but it can be helpful to follow relevant people, groups, and organizations.

Make the Most of Your LinkedIn Profile

As you're finishing your profile, proof for errors and visual appeal, create a custom URL, and make sure your profile is publicly visible. Proof your LinkedIn profile carefully for errors on mobile devices and computers. Make sure it looks great on smart phones, tablets, and computers.

Make it easier for clients to find you with a custom LinkedIn URL. This also makes you look more professional. To create a custom URL click Edit public profile on the right. Scroll down to Edit Your Custom URL. Click the edit button. Add your name after linkedin.com/in/.

If you want clients to find you on LinkedIn, make sure your profile is switched on for public visibility. To do this, click Edit public profile on the right, scroll down to Edit Visibility, and click the on switch.

BONUS CONTENT

Tool: The Ultimate LinkedIn Profile Checklist for Freelancers

Tool: The Ultimate Guide to LinkedIn for Freelancers

Get the bonus content:
www.themightymarketer.com/bonus-fearless-freelancer

Key Takeaways

Here's a quick summary of the key takeaways from Step 7:

- More clients are searching for freelancers on LinkedIn.

- A complete, client-focused profile will help you attract clients and impress colleagues—even in a recession.

- The keys to attracting steady, high-paying clients on LinkedIn are a client-focused headline and About section, both with the right keywords.

- Your LinkedIn profile isn't a resume. Include just enough key content—and the right content—so that clients know that you're the right choice for them. Be interesting and conversational.

In Step 8, we'll cover the other key part of your online presence: your website. Step 9, on networking, will cover how to build your LinkedIn network and use it effectively.

Step 8. Create a Client-Focused Website

"Marketing is a contest for people's attention."
— Seth Godin

Thrive by Impressing Clients with Your Website

Just as clients expect freelancers to be on LinkedIn, they expect us to have websites too. An awesome, client-focused website shows clients that you're the right choice for them and shows colleagues that you're a professional who will do a great job if they refer work to you. In Step 8, you'll learn how to:

- Identify the essential web pages for freelancers
- Develop web content to attract more clients with less marketing
- Choose a website design that helps you communicate effectively
- Work with a professional web designer
- Avoid common pitfalls in freelance websites.

Create an Awesome, Client-Focused Website

An awesome, client-focused website will:

- Impress clients and colleagues by showing them you understand client needs
- Highlight your expertise, skills, and work (usually through samples)
- Show that you're a professional who is running a business.

Do Less Marketing

If you have a client-focused website, you'll be able to do less marketing—because your website will do the work for you. When clients contact you, they'll already know a lot about you and your services. So you won't have to actively "sell yourself," the part of marketing that freelancers hate most.

Whether you're creating your first freelance website or updating your website, remember that clients only care about how you can help them meet their needs. Your website content needs to quickly tell them:

- What you do (your services)
- Who you do it for (your target clients)
- How what you do benefits clients.

Getting the attention of clients fast is key. When people view a website, they spend about 50 milliseconds (0.05 second) deciding whether they like it and will stay or leave, according to a study published in Behavior & Information Technology.

Your content and design need to work together to clearly show how you help clients. If your freelance website doesn't do this—and many freelance websites don't—the client will quickly reject you and move on to the next freelancer on their list.

Create an Awesome Freelance Website

You only need two things to attract steady, high-paying clients with your website: Content that's compelling, clear, and focused on client needs and design that's amazing (visually engaging, clear, and easy to navigate).

Use your client-focused marketing messages from Step 2 to create awesome content, and your brand to create amazing design. Read the rest of this step. Then go back and work on your brand statement and marketing messages.

If you already have a freelance website, it might be time for an update. Website design and content change. And most freelance businesses evolve over time.

Here's what you need to do to attract steady, high-paying clients and get more referrals from colleagues—even in a recession:

- Focus on client needs
- Be compelling
- Be clear
- Write scannable content
- Include the essential content for freelancers.

If you already have a client-focused LinkedIn profile, you should have much of the information you need for your web content.

BONUS CONTENT

Tool: Awesome Freelance Website Checklist (for website content, writing, and design)

Get the bonus content:
www.themightymarketer.com/bonus-fearless-freelancer

Write Compelling, Clear, and Client-Focused Content

Use client-focused marketing messages, include the essential web pages for freelancers, and write conversational, concise, and scannable content.

Compel Clients with Key Messages

Use your key client-focused marketing messages in your banner heads, banner subheads, blurbs (brief descriptions), and other subheads to highlight the benefits clients get when they work with you. A banner is the horizontal bar near the top of every web page on many modern website designs.

Include the Essential Web Pages for Freelancers

These are the essential web pages for freelancers:

- Home
- About
- Services
- Samples, Portfolio, or Work
- Testimonials, Clients, or Testimonials and Clients
- Contact.

You can combine and organize Services; Portfolio, Samples, or Work; and Testimonials, Clients, or Testimonials and Clients in different ways. I cover this below.

Your Home Page

Together, your Home page content and design quickly answer the only question that clients really care about: What's In It For Me? Your Home page tells them:

- What you do (your services)
- Who you do it for (your target clients)
- How what you do benefits clients.

You'll draft your Home page last. But you should be thinking about your Home page as you write the rest of your content.

A compelling, client-focused freelance website Home page includes:

- A header banner with your key message and a subhead (or blurb)
- Images that contribute to your key messages (or no images)
- Shortcut boxes
- A clear call to action with your contact information
- A design that's optimized for multiple screens.

Logos and a banner are relevant, effective images for a freelancer's Home page. A logo is a visual way to represent your business (Step 2). A tagline is a memorable phrase or sentence that helps your target clients understand what you do.

If you don't have a logo and want one, your web designer should be able to help you develop one or refer you to a designer who specializes in logo design.

A banner is a great way to highlight your key message on your Home page and quickly tell clients what they want to know. It supports both client-focused content and amazing design. The banner on your Home page is usually bigger than the banner on the other pages.

Make sure that any image you include in your banner is relevant and that your key message is clear. Freelance writers and editors often have banner images that obscure their key message, because they're not designers. Sometimes the images they use make no sense.

Either of these problems will drive clients away—in less than the blink of an eye. Hiring a professional designer, which I cover below, will prevent this problem.

Home page shortcut boxes add more visual appeal to a website and let you highlight key content quickly. Each shortcut box is linked to a page on your website. You can use up to about 30 characters (with spaces) in the headline of a shortcut box and up to about 115 characters (with spaces) in each blurb.

Make it easy for clients to contact you with a clear call to action, your contact information, and a link to your Contact page. A call to action says what you want clients to do, for example, "Call or email me today." The bar at the bottom of your Home page (and every page) is a great place for your call to action and contact information.

More and more people are using smart phones and tablets to view websites. Data can be slower on mobile devices and how fast your website loads matters. A professional website designer will take care of this for you and provide other technical assistance.

About

Start the About page with one to three sentences about how the client would benefit by working with you. Then, briefly include the most relevant (to clients) information about your:

- Experience
- Education
- Awards and honors
- Other professional accomplishments.

If you want to provide more information, link to a subpage with your resume or a longer bio. Include a professional headshot.

Services

Services is an easy page to write. Select categories based on the type of work you do and use bulleted lists for services under each category. So sample categories could include:

- Services (e.g., writing, editing, consulting, publication management, and training)

- Projects (e.g., articles, blogs, continuing medical education, white papers, newsletters, social media, and web content)
- Areas of expertise, topic areas, or therapeutic areas (e.g., cardiovascular disease, cancer, diabetes; banking and financial planning).

Samples, Portfolio, or Work

This is another easy page to write. If you have samples you can share, use categories that make it easy for clients to find what they're most interested in. Also use categories that let you highlight the type of work you most want to do.

If your work is proprietary, instead of samples, use a project list and/or brief project descriptions to show what you've done. Write about what you've done and the type of clients you work with without mentioning names of clients or specific projects.

If you're a new freelancer, put a little information about your work on your Services page instead of having a separate page for this. Add a few paragraphs with some project descriptions and/or use samples like:

- LinkedIn articles
- Volunteer work for professional associations
- School projects
- Spec samples (a speculative sample that's like a project you want to work on).

Clients and Testimonials

The Clients content is also easy to develop. Choose categories that let you highlight your most important services and interests, such as industries or types of work. Or just list your clients. Using a partial list of clients, under a subhead Sample Clients or Select Clients is a good idea.

If you're a new freelancer, you won't have a Clients page yet. That's fine. Add it when you're ready. If you only have a few clients, instead of a separate page, add a Sample Clients section on your Services page.

What others say about you is far more powerful than what you say about yourself. Testimonials from satisfied clients help you attract more clients—because new clients want to know that other clients value your work.

You can combine Testimonials with Clients on one page, have two separate pages, or sprinkle testimonials throughout your website.

If you're a new freelancer, you won't have testimonials, or enough testimonials for a separate page yet. If you have one to three testimonials, sprinkle them throughout your website. Add a Testimonials page when you have about five testimonials.

Contact Information

Make it easy for clients to get in touch with you with contact information that's easy to find. Use a simple Contact page. Include your name, email address, and phone number. I recommend that you also include your city and state, to help show that you're running a real business.

Start your Contact page with a call to action (what you want the client to do). A call to action starts with a phrase or sentence that urges the prospect to take action now, like "Contact me today."

And include your email address and phone number on every page. The bottom of each page is a great place for this.

Write for the Web

Writing web content is very different than other types of writing. Web users:

- Scan, reading only 20%-28% of the average web page
- Stay on an average page less than a minute
- Often stay on a web page 10 seconds or less

So if clients don't find what they need on your website fast, they'll leave—and move on to the next freelancer on their list.

Be Conversational, Concise, and Scannable

Along with compelling, clear, and client-focused content, you need to write for the Web:

- Write like you're having a conversation with someone.

- Put your key marketing messages and other important information first.
- Be concise.
- Use banners, heads, and subheads to make your content scannable and help convey your key marketing messages.
- Keep paragraphs short and sentences simple. On the Web, a one-sentence paragraph is fine.
- Use simple, familiar words that your target clients understand.
- Avoid jargon, and avoid or limit acronyms and abbreviations.
- Use the active voice and lots of verbs.
- Use bulleted lists, where appropriate.

BONUS CONTENT
How to Win High-Paying Clients with Your Freelance Website
Get the bonus content:
www.themightymarketer.com/bonus-fearless-freelancer

Highlight Your Content with a Professional Design

If your content is compelling but your design isn't visually engaging and clear, clients will move on to the other freelancers on their list. Here's the truth. Many websites of freelance writers and editors have awful designs.

These websites look like they were designed by an amateur—because they were. Templates in drag-and-drop website builders like Squarespace, Weebly, or Wix make it seem like it's very easy to design your own website. But if you don't have knowledge of good design and the technical ability to adapt templates to a freelancer's needs, your website will be amateurish.

Don't Drive Away Clients

Often, freelancers design their own websites because they think it's cheaper than hiring a professional designer. But it may not be. If you don't know what you're doing, then it's cheaper to hire a designer—because you'll lose a lot of billable time by trying to design your own website. And you can't put a price tag on the clients you'll lose if your freelance website drives clients away.

Work with a professional website designer who has experience working with freelancers. Your designer will create a customized, visually engaging website for you. He/she will know how to modify templates to your needs and incorporate your brand to help you stand out in a sea of freelancers.

You'll get back the upfront cost of paying for a designer many times over because your website will help you get steady, high-paying clients. And your designer can help you with the technical aspects of launching your website and dealing with those inevitable tech issues.

Key Elements in Freelance Website Design

Some elements of compelling web content, like heads and subheads, also contribute to amazing web design. Head and subheads let you use words and design to grab the attention of your target clients fast. Focus your heads and subheads on the needs of your clients and how you meet those needs. Clearly and concisely say what you do and how this benefits clients.

Other key design elements are:

- Images that help you convey your key messages, instead of leaving clients wondering why they're on your website
- Design that looks good on different screen sizes (smart phones, tablets, and computers)
- Home page shortcut boxes
- Fonts that are easy to read online
- Colors that create balance and harmony, and make reading online easy

- Design that loads quickly, so you don't lose clients
- Easy-to-find contact information and a clear call to action.

How to Work with a Professional Website Designer

Getting recommendations from people you know and trust is the best way to find a professional website designer. When you see a freelancer's website that you like, email him/her to ask who designed it. Also ask about your colleague's experience working with the designer. Some designers are very talented, but they don't listen to what you want.

Stay away from sites like fiverr when you look for a website designer. While the low price may seem attractive, your website won't be customized to your business, and it won't be nearly as effective in attracting high-paying clients.

Website designers know what makes good and bad design. So treat your website designer with respect and listen to his/her advice. But also be firm about what works best for a freelance business. For example, some designers insist on including a contact form and a blog, because business websites are "supposed" to have these features. Just say no.

Sometimes designers insist on a certain theme or design features because that's the way they always do things. If it's not what you want, just say no.

Be honest about what you like and don't like when you're working with your designer. Otherwise, you won't get the website you want.

BONUS CONTENT

Tool: Awesome Freelance Website Template for working with a designer

Why You Need a Website Designer

Get the bonus content:
www.themightymarketer.com/bonus-fearless-freelancer

Avoid Common Pitfalls in Freelance Websites

Web designers and gurus push everyone to use images on the Home page, have a blog, use a contact form, and focus on SEO (search engine optimization). While these things are crucial for many types of businesses and organizations, none of them are necessary for freelancers. Some of them are actually harmful.

Home Page Image(s)

You can have one or more images on your Home page, but you don't need images. If an image doesn't contribute to your message, it doesn't belong on your Home page—or anywhere on your website. It will just confuse clients and drive them away.

Don't let a designer convince you that you need images, or add images yourself because the template has a space for them. Don't use images because you see them on other freelancers' websites because many of these websites are awful.

A logo is one type of image that does belong on your Home page and every page of your website. If you don't have a logo and want one, work with a designer to develop this so you can use it on your website.

Blog

A key purpose of a blog is to continually provide fresh web content and increase rankings in search results. But clients won't be searching the Web for you, so you don't need to worry about search results. And they aren't likely to read your blog.

Many freelancers start a blog, write a few posts, and then ignore it. Imagine a client who does see your blog and finds a few posts from a year ago. That client will quickly move on to the next freelancer. A blog just isn't worth the time and effort that's necessary to do it right.

Contact Form

Yes, I'm repeating myself here because this is so important. Web designers almost always insist on a contact form and web templates include them. Just say no!

A contact form implies that someone will get back to you eventually. When a client decides to hire or consider you, he/she almost always wants to reach you fast.

And a contact form is impersonal. As freelancers, we need to build relationships with clients, not annoy them. Contact forms may be necessary for corporations and other big organizations, but they're never appropriate for, or helpful to, freelancers.

SEO

Don't worry about SEO, which involves writing web content that Google and other search engines will find and rank highly in search results. The goal of SEO is to increase the number of visitors to a website.

But clients rarely, if ever, search the Web for freelancers. If they did, they'd get so many results that they'd never wade through them. Clients who want to do a general search for freelancers will use LinkedIn, a professional association directory, or a forum for freelancers.

As freelancers, we need to drive traffic to our websites through our other marketing. Your website is there to persuade the client to contact or hire you after they've heard about you through direct email, networking, or a referral. In my view, there's no reason to spend any time, effort, or money on SEO, which changes constantly.

Use Your Website to Market Your Business

Put your URL on all marketing materials, including your email signature, LinkedIn profile, and business cards. Including your website on your LinkedIn profile is very effective because a client who's reading your profile is just one click away from your website. Make sure you put your URL under Contact info in your introduction card and again in About.

Updates

Once your website is live, you won't need to spend much time or effort maintaining it. Review your website at least quarterly and make any necessary updates. Add new samples or project descriptions. Update anything that's not current. Every January, change the year of the website (if this isn't automatic on your platform) and make all other necessary quantitative updates (e.g., years in business).

Key Takeaways

Here's a quick summary of the key takeaways from Step 8:

- An awesome, client-focused website will help you attract more clients with less marketing.

- Your Home page—the most important part of your website—needs to clearly describe what you do and who you do it for.

- Compelling web content is conversational, concise, and scannable. Key marketing messages focus on client needs.

- Do-it-yourself websites drive away clients. Freelance writers and editors need to hire a web designer.

- Most general advice about websites isn't applicable to freelancers, and some of it can damage your reputation:

- Don't use images unless they help convey key messages.

- You don't need a blog.

- Never use a contact form.

- Don't worry about SEO.

Step 9 covers how to meet people who can help and hire you and how to build a strong network.

Step 9. Meet People Who Can Help and Hire You

"If people like you they'll listen to you, but if they trust you, they'll do business with you."
— Zig Ziglar

Thrive by Building Your Network

Who you know—a.k.a. your network—can be more important than anything else in getting steady, high-paying clients. Having a strong, trusting network is even more important in a recession. In Step 9, you'll learn how to:

- Make networking fun, not stressful or scary
- Build a strategic network
- Get more referrals
- Network effectively in person and virtually.

Make Networking Fun, Not Stressful or Scary

If you're like most freelancers, networking is stressful—even scary. Many of us are shy. We like to work alone and usually dread leaving the safe cocoon of our offices to go to a networking event. Even virtual networking can feel uncomfortable.

But you need a strong, strategic network because clients use networking to find freelancers they can trust. If you're not in their network or the network of someone they know, they can't find you.

With the right networking attitude and some knowledge about what works best, networking will be easier and less stressful. It can even be fun. And like other marketing, the more you practice, the easier it will be.

Develop the Right Networking Attitude

Most freelancers, including me when I was starting out, don't understand networking. So we have a bad attitude about it. And this makes networking harder for us. Once you understand networking, you'll become more comfortable doing it. And you'll get better at it.

Here's the truth. Networking isn't about "selling yourself." It's about getting to know people. Trying to sell your services—what we think we're supposed to do—doesn't work. And it's very stressful.

But when you focus on getting to know people, networking is so much easier! You're listening to the other person/people and asking questions. The pressure is off.

Give More than You Take

Giving more than you take is my golden rule of networking for freelancers. When you focus on getting to know other people and helping them without expecting anything in return, networking is so much easier.

And there's proof that this works. In his best-selling book *Give and Take*, Wharton Management Professor Adam Grant reported that people who give their time, knowledge, ideas, and connections to others without expecting anything in return ("givers") are more successful than people who think it's a dog-eat-dog world and focus only on self-promotion ("takers"). Grant's research shows that nice guys (and gals) can finish first, not last.

By giving, we build trust and establish our credibility. The result, over time, is more referrals and more new clients. Ways to give include sending links to useful content, connecting colleagues to other people who can help them, and referring other freelancers to clients.

The Little-Known Personality Type that Makes Networking Easier

Being an introvert makes networking scary and harder. But most freelancers who think they're introverts are actually ambiverts. Ambiverts are part introvert and part extrovert. It's easier for us to network than it is for introverts or extroverts because we know when to talk and when to listen. Introverts are too quiet and extroverts talk too much. But ambiverts are just right.

Find out what you are by looking up online and taking The Quiet Revolution Personality Test. Even if you find out you are an introvert, a little attitude adjustment can make networking easier for you.

Build a Strategic Network

Be nice to everyone you meet, but be strategic about how—and where—you spend most of your networking time. Focus on the people and places that will be most useful to you. But remember to give more to them than you take from them.

Spend most of your networking time and effort building relationships with the people who you think can become part of your strategic network, not meeting lots of new people briefly.

Focus on Other Freelancers

Make other freelancers a key part of your strategic network. They're a great source of advice and support, along with referrals.

Other freelancers can help you learn what to do—and what not to do—in running your freelance business. They can help you handle difficult clients and decide whether a freelance opportunity is right for you. And they can provide support when things aren't going well and celebrate successes with you.

Go to the Right Places

Go to places where clients are likely to look for your type of freelancer, especially professional associations. You can do some strategic networking online through LinkedIn, social networks of professional associations, and other online forums for freelancers. But in-person networking is best for building strong relationships when you can do it.

Tap into the Power of Referrals

Word of mouth, a.k.a. referrals, is really powerful. In my 2019 survey of how freelancers market their services, freelancers said that word of mouth was the #1 source of their best clients. Other surveys of freelancers and other small business owners have shown similar results.

Yet, just 33% of freelancers surveyed said they get at least 51% of their business from referrals. And 12% of freelancers get less than 25% of their business from referrals.

Freelancers get referrals from satisfied clients and colleagues. When you do great work, clients will start to refer you to their colleagues, within their organization and at other organizations. This step focuses on referrals from colleagues, especially other freelancers.

Be Active in Professional Associations

Professional associations are the easiest way to get referrals because they're full of people who are working your specialty(ies). You'll meet colleagues and other freelancers who can refer work to you—and prospective clients too. When clients need freelancers they can trust, they often ask colleagues in their professional associations for recommendations.

Build Trust Fast by Volunteering

Volunteering for your professional associations is the quickest way to build the trusting relationships that lead to referrals, and to impress the prospective clients you meet. And if you're like most freelancers, volunteering is much easier than other types of networking.

Look for information about volunteering on the websites of your professional associations. If you don't find it, just email one of the officers and say that you'd like to volunteer. By joining and being active in professional associations, you'll also be able to learn about your ideal clients and find ideal clients for your marketing.

Find the Right Professional Associations

Ask your freelance friends and your clients which professional associations they belong to and would recommend. Use the Directory of Associations to search for professional associations.

Before joining a professional association, check out the website and available resources, and try to go to a meeting or conference. Sometimes though, you just have to join a professional association for a year and see what you think.

Master Networking Events

Meeting people in person at networking events is the best way to begin to build strong, trusting relationships. And people won't hire you or refer work to you unless they trust you. Networking events are especially important for meeting other freelancers.

Conferences let you make lots of key contacts in a few days and deepen relationships with current key contacts. And, of course, the conference content helps you stay updated with your industry or field and learn things to better manage your freelance business.

Networking events don't have to be scary. If you prepare before the event, and do the right things during the event, it will be much easier—and more effective. To build a strategic network, you also need to do the right things after the event.

Before the Networking Event

Prepare for the networking event by knowing how you'll introduce yourself, bringing business cards, and dressing to impress clients and colleagues. Your elevator speech is what you say so that people understand—in 30 seconds or less—what you do and how you help your clients. Include:

- The benefit clients get when they work with you
- What you do (your services)
- Who you work with (type of clients).

Your business card is a powerful ad for your business—and a way for people to remember you. Make sure your cards are clear, high-quality, and error-free. And make sure you have a complete, client-focused LinkedIn profile and/or website to impress the people you're meeting when they check you out later.

How you dress for networking matters—a lot. People form opinions about you within a few seconds, based on your appearance.

And when you look good, you boost your self-esteem. This makes networking easier. Business casual works for most networking events, unless your clients and industry require more professional dress.

During the Networking Event

Go to the networking event with a positive attitude. Focus on giving more than you take.

Smile. This will relax you and make it easier for other people to talk to you. Pay attention to how you look and sound when you meet people. This matters much more than what you say.

How much someone likes you, according to research by Albert Mehrabian, professor emeritus of psychology at UCLA, depends on:

- Appearance and body language: about 55%
- Tone, volume, and cadence of voice: about 38%
- What you say: just 7%.
- Talk to people

Most people will be happy if you talk to them. Many, especially other freelancers, are shy. So be brave, and do this yourself. Talk to people who you meet in line and people you sit next to at a presentation, session, or meal.

Prepare what you'll say when you first meet someone. Here are a few ideas:

- Why did you decide to come to this conference?
- What sessions are you attending?
- How did you come to be a [WHATEVER THE PERSON DOES]?
- What do you like best about your work?

You can also start a conversation by mentioning something about the person or simply saying hi:

- Wow, I love your [NECKLACE, TIE, ETC].

- "Hi. I don't think we've met before. I'm Lori."
- Know how to end a conversation.

Ending a conversation is harder than starting one. Here are some nice ways to do this:

- It's been so nice talking to you! Do you have a card?
- I don't want to keep you from everyone else, but let's connect. Here's my card.
- I need to run to my session. Take care!

Take breaks when you need to. Being around other people all day can be exhausting for freelancers who are used to working alone.

Be reasonable about what you expect to get out of networking events. You're not going to leave the event with a bunch of new clients. The real results of networking come from building relationships with people after the event.

After the Networking Event

Follow up and stay in touch regularly with the people you're meeting. That's where the real results of networking will come from. Soon after the event, follow up with people you think could be helpful to you (and you to them). Do this by inviting each person to join your LinkedIn network and/or sending an email to say "nice to meet you."

Stay in touch with your new contacts and key contacts you already know regularly so that:

- Clients think of you first when they need a freelancer
- Colleagues think of you first when they have freelance work to share.

Be polite and professional, and focus mostly on providing your contacts with useful information and resources. Once or twice a year, mention your freelance services.

Step 10 will give you more information about follow-up.

BONUS CONTENT
Tool: The Ultimate Networking Event Checklist for Freelancers
12 Ways to Make Networking Events Amazing, Not Scary
Get the bonus content:
www.themightymarketer.com/bonus-fearless-freelancer

Master Virtual Networking

While I doubt that virtual networking will ever be as helpful as in-person networking, it's likely to become more popular as a result of the pandemic. Also, virtual networking takes a lot less time than attending live conferences and other networking events.

Great ways for freelancers to network virtually include LinkedIn, social networks of professional associations, and forums for freelancers. Like in-person networking, focus on giving more than you take in virtual networking.

Networking on LinkedIn

LinkedIn is becoming a more popular way for freelancers to network. Having a big, relevant network (500+ connections) and being active on LinkedIn help you:

- Rank higher in search results when clients are looking for freelancers
- Showcase your expertise to clients and colleagues
- Build your network of freelancers who can provide advice and support
- Learn how to better manage your business.

Of the top five criteria LinkedIn uses in providing search results, common connections with the person who is doing the search is #2. So having at least 500 relevant connections really helps you rank high in search results when clients are looking for freelancers.

And a network of 500 relevant connections could give you access to at least 250,000 people, including lots of potential clients. Relevant connections are:

- Clients
- Other freelancers you know
- Freelancers and other colleagues from your professional associations you haven't met yet
- Other people working in your industry(ies) or target markets.

If you don't know a lot of people yet, don't worry. By being active (covered next), you'll meet relevant people you can invite to connect with you.

LinkedIn has three levels of connections: 1st, 2nd, and 3rd degree. The closer your connections are with the person who is doing the search, the higher you'll rank in search results.

1st-degree connections are direct connections. Either you invited the person to connect with you or he/she invited you to connect with him/her. 1st-degree connections:

- See each other's connections (usually; this depends on the settings each person uses)
- Can send direct messages for free
- Automatically follow each other.

Following means that you will see some of their content, and they will see some of yours. LinkedIn has a very complicated algorithm for deciding which content to show you. If you want to keep seeing a connection's content, comment on it regularly.

2nd-degree connections are connections of your 1st-degree connections. Having access to these people can give you a huge network. Say that you have 500 1st-degree connections, who each have 500 1st-degree connections. Your network is now 250,000 connections.

3rd-degree connections are people who are connected to your 2nd-degree connections. If their first and last names show on their profile, you can click Connect to invite them to be part of your network. If only the first letter of their last name shows, you won't have an option to click Connect. You can't message them for free.

Always Send Personal Invitations

Always add a personal note when you invite someone to connect with you. Mention what you have in common or why you want to connect. For example, you could write:

"I see we're both freelance writers and I'd love to connect with you on LinkedIn."

OR

"I loved your post on XYZ. Please join my LinkedIn network."

If the person is a potential client, mention something about his/her career or company or something you have in common (like graduating from the same college).

Never click Connect under People You May Know. LinkedIn will automatically send the default invite. Instead, search for the person by name and click on his/her profile. Then click Connect, and LinkedIn will prompt you to add a personal note.

LinkedIn's mobile app doesn't prompt you to add a personal note to connection invites. But there's an easy way to do this. Search for the person you want to invite. Click More. Click Personalize invite.

Be Active

Of the top five criteria LinkedIn uses in providing search results, activity is #4. Activity means sharing content and engaging with other people on your content and their content. Always be professional on LinkedIn.

Once you get used to sharing and engaging, it only takes about 20 minutes a day (Monday through Friday) to get results. Review your LinkedIn feed—the content that shows up when you click on your LinkedIn Home page—2-3 times a day. Comment on relevant posts by relevant people. And you don't have to do this every day. If you're super busy, it's okay to skip a day or two.

About once or twice a week, do your own posts. There are three types of content you can share: posts, articles, and videos. In general, posts are just as good as articles for ranking in search results and building your network.

But articles can help you highlight your expertise. When you publish an article, it becomes part of your LinkedIn profile. And you can send links to your articles to clients, prospective clients, and freelance friends. Focus on topics that are relevant to your target clients.

I'm not covering videos because I think it's just way too much work to do the high-quality videos that should be shared on social media. But if videos would benefit your specific freelance business and you know how to produce high-quality videos, by all means use them.

If you're not very active on LinkedIn yet, start by engaging with other people before sharing your own content. There are three ways to engage with other people: like, comment, or share.

Commenting is the best way to engage others, and it's easy to do. Just read the post and write a meaningful comment. Look for relevant posts by relevant people, like potential clients and other freelancers, to comment on.

Every comment is a mini-ad for your business because your name and the beginning of your headline show before your comment, along with your photo. This is one of the reasons why you need a compelling, client-focused headline (Step 6).

Once you're comfortable on LinkedIn, share relevant content in posts once or twice a week. Relevant content includes:

- News and updates about your industry or specialty(ies)
- Tips on being more productive
- Other useful free content like blog posts, podcasts, and webinars.

In your post include at least a few sentences about the content, usually with a link to the full content (news, blog post, etc.). Use an image to increase the number of views and engagement.

Sign up for e-newsletters, and you'll have a steady stream of content ideas coming to your inbox. Professional associations are also a great source of relevant content you can share. You can also use this content to follow up with interested clients, clients, and freelance friends (Step 10).

Most of what you share should be non-promotional. When you do promote something related to your freelance work, make sure it's relevant to your connections.

Increase engagement by responding to every comment people make on your posts. Very few people do this, so if you do, you'll stand out. And people who comment on your posts are likely to accept an invite to connect from you.

BONUS CONTENT

How to Be Active and Effective on LinkedIn Even if You Hate Social Media

Get the bonus content:
www.themightymarketer.com/bonus-fearless-freelancer

Other Social Networks

The basic principles of building a relevant network and sharing useful content are the same for LinkedIn, social networks of professional associations (sometimes called online communities), and forums for freelancers. But these social networks and forums have more rules and guidelines than LinkedIn.

On LinkedIn, more than modest self-promotion and asking for business is bad. On other social networks and forums, it's not allowed. Members are supposed to share and solicit advice and provide information that other members can use.

Here are two rules from two different professional association online communities I'm part of:

- "Do not self-promote any individual, company, product, or service."
- "Do not post self-promotional messages, including offering services and seeking jobs (whether paid or unpaid)."

Key Takeaways

Here's a quick summary of the key takeaways from Step 9:

- Clients use networking to find freelancers they can trust. If you're not in their network or the network of someone they know, they can't find you.

- Networking doesn't have to be stressful or scary. It's about getting to know people, not selling yourself. When you focus on getting to know people and helping them without expecting anything in return, networking is much easier.

- Referrals are the easiest way to get steady, high-paying clients. Get more referrals by networking through professional associations and building a trusting network of other freelancers.

- Meeting people in person is the best way to begin to build strong, trusting relationships. Conferences let you make lots of key contacts in a few days and deepen relationships with current key contacts.

- Virtual networking is likely to become more popular as a result of the pandemic. Great ways for freelancers to network virtually include LinkedIn, social networks or online communities of professional associations, and forums for freelancers.

In Step 10, I'll show you how to stay in touch with interested clients who haven't yet hired you (and current clients) and freelance friends so they think of you first when they need a freelancer or have freelance work to refer.

Step 10. Be First in Line for Freelance Work

"The ladder of success is best climbed by stepping on
the rungs of opportunity."
— Ayn Rand

Thrive by Creating Top-of-Mind Awareness

Up to 90% of the time, clients aren't ready to hire a freelancer
when you first contact them. If you follow up with interested
clients, you'll be first in line when they are ready to hire a
freelancer. With fewer clients hiring freelancers in a recession,
follow-up is more important than ever. Staying in touch with
current clients and colleagues also helps you get more freelance
work. In Step 10, you'll learn how to:

- Get high-paying clients by making sure that clients think
  of you first when they're looking to hire a freelancer and
  colleagues think of you first when they have work to
  refer

- Stay in touch with interested clients, inactive clients, and
  colleagues, especially other freelancers, without selling
  yourself

- Develop a list of your interested clients, current clients,
  inactive clients, and colleagues and a plan for targeted
  follow-up—so you can get more steady, high-paying
  clients.

Use Targeted Follow-Up

Many freelancers miss out on getting steady, high-paying
clients because they never or rarely follow up with clients who've
expressed interest in their services but haven't hired them. The
single most important thing you can do to get these clients is to
stay in touch with them regularly.

Here's why. Freelancers provide B2B (business to business)
services. Even if your clients are non-profit organizations,

universities, or other organizations that aren't businesses, the B2B rules still apply.

How Clients Buy Freelance Services

Clients rarely buy B2B services the first time they hear from a freelancer (or any business). That's why sending one direct email and hoping that the client will hire you someday rarely works—even if the client said they were interested in your services. Marketing Charts says that 74.6% of customers take at least 4 months to buy a service or product and 46.4% take 7 months or more.

Most salespeople—79%—give up somewhere between the first and second follow-up, says Josh Turner in *The Trust Equation*. Now, I know freelancers aren't salespeople. Salespeople are trained in selling, and they like to do this. We don't. Even if 79% of freelancers give up after one or two contacts—and I'm sure the percentage is much higher—that's good news for you. If you follow up, you'll stand out.

Be First in Line When Clients Need a Freelancer

Clients who say they'll put you in their freelance database or keep you in mind for future freelance jobs aren't lying to you or blowing you off. They just don't need freelance help right now.

These clients are likely to hire you within a year or so if they think of you first when they're ready to hire a freelancer. Here are two of my stories.

A few years ago, I worked on a big project for an Ivy League nursing school. It was so big that I had to bring in three other freelancers to help me. My contact there was someone I had worked with at another organization. He had been on my follow-up list for about a year when he called me.

After the project ended, he called me "an absolute pleasure to work with" and told me that he "couldn't be happier with the final product." But he didn't need any more freelance help.

I kept him on my e-newsletter list and sent him a card at the holidays. Two years later, when a colleague at the nursing school needed help with another big project, he referred them to me. The colleague hired me after one email because she trusted the referral from my contact.

Another client, who I've been working with since 1998, hired me nearly two years after he first said he wanted to work with me. Between my first contact with this client and when he hired me, I had been following up regularly. Other freelancers who follow up regularly have similar stories.

Also follow up regularly with current and inactive clients and colleagues, especially other freelancers. Following up with current and inactive clients can lead to more freelance work.

And staying in touch with colleagues can lead to referrals. When I hear about a freelance opportunity that's not right for me, the freelancers I think of first for the referral are those who have been in touch with me most often and most recently.

BONUS CONTENT
The Surprising Thing that Will Get You More Freelance Work: Follow-Up
Get the bonus content:
www.themightymarketer.com/bonus-fearless-freelancer

Do Professional and Targeted Follow-Up

With fewer clients hiring freelancers in a recession, what I call targeted follow-up is more important than ever. If your follow-up is professional, you won't be bothering or annoying anyone. Clients often appreciate the follow-up because they need great freelancers—even if they didn't need you when you first contacted them.

One of my new clients recently thanked me for following up with him (for the third time) because he had "a million things going on." Keeping in touch helped him remember that he wanted to work with me.

An Easy and Efficient Way to Get Clients

Targeted follow-up isn't about selling yourself. In fact, most of the time, you shouldn't even mention your freelance services.

And it doesn't take long. Depending on how many people you're following up with, targeted follow-up should take you about two to five hours a month.

Most of your follow-up should be customized to the client organization or your contact person, or your freelance friend. Commenting on news is an easy way to do customized follow-up about clients or the contact person.

Ways to find news to comment on include Google alerts, the company's Newsroom page, and LinkedIn posts. Another easy way to customize follow-up is by sharing relevant content like blog posts, reports, and podcasts. And while you'll send the content to each contact person individually, you can usually use the same content for multiple contacts.

Sharing relevant content is a great way to follow up with freelance friends too. And if your freelance friends do similar work, you can send the same content individually to multiple freelancers.

Sign up for e-newsletters in your industry(ies) and target markets so this content comes right to your inbox and you don't have to waste time searching for it. Also use this content in LinkedIn posts (Step 9).

Generic follow-up—sending the same thing to everyone—works too. Developing your own e-newsletter is a great way to follow up with everyone on your list at the same time. Most of the content in an e-newsletter is useful and relevant, not promotional.

An e-newsletter lets you highlight your expertise and preferred work. For example, I love doing content marketing for hospitals, healthcare marketing agencies, etc. The feature story in a recent issue of my e-newsletter, Engage!, focused on why patients don't understand health content. The story shows that I understand patients and can help my clients communicate with them.

BONUS CONTENT

11 Steps to a Remarkable E-Newsletter that Will Impress Clients

Why You Need to Have an Email Newsletter

Get all bonus content:
www.themightymarketer.com/bonus-fearless-freelancer

Generic follow-up also includes holiday cards. These should be print cards that arrive in the mail shortly after Thanksgiving—before cards start getting lost in the holiday rush.

A Friendly Reminder About Your Freelance Services

Once or twice a year, it's fine to send interested clients and inactive clients a friendly reminder that you're available for freelance work. But this must be part of your follow-up process and not the only time you contact these clients. Send a professional, low-key email.

You can also send a similar email to your freelance friends. Let them know what type of work you're looking for and ask about what type of work they're looking for. Only do this as part of your follow-up process.

Develop Your Simple Follow-Up Process

Now you know how to follow up with interested clients, current clients, inactive clients, and freelance friends. Next, you need to develop a simple process to make it easy to follow up regularly. Consistent follow-up requires three things: (1) Developing a list, (2) Scheduling the time, and (3) Developing your content library.

Put your targeted follow-up list in a tracker with a schedule for following up. You can do your tracker in a spreadsheet, a database, a Word document, or any other format that works for you. Record each follow-up, and any response you get, in your tracker.

Mark time for follow-up on your calendar—and treat it like a deadline for a client. Get it done.

Block out 30-60 minutes a week to look for news and review content for your content library (covered below) and 2-4 hours a month for following up with people (depending on how many people are on your list). Here's what I recommend for your follow-up schedule:

- Interested clients: About every 2 months
- Inactive clients: About every 3 months
- Clients: About every 3-5 months if you're working with them regularly
- Freelance friends and other colleagues: About every 3-4 months

---

BONUS CONTENT
Tool: Targeted Follow-Up Tracker (Spreadsheet)
Get all bonus content:
www.themightymarketer.com/bonus-fearless-freelancer

Having a content library ensures that you'll have lots of content (blog posts, reports, podcasts, etc.) ready when you need it. Stock your library (a folder on your computer with the content or a list of links to content) with:

- E-newsletters that are relevant to your clients
- Relevant LinkedIn updates (I get lots of content for follow-up through LinkedIn)
- Resources from your professional associations.

If something is timely, like an upcoming webinar, send it along right away. Otherwise, file it away for your scheduled follow-up.

Review Your Follow-Up Results

At least once a year, review your targeted follow-up list. Many experts recommend staying in touch with people for about two years. If you haven't received any response from an interested or inactive client after that, you can take the person off your list.

But there are many stories about freelancers who got a steady, high-paying client after years of follow-up. So if you really want to work with a particular client who hasn't responded to your targeted follow-up, it may be worthwhile to keep that client on your list.

Add new interested clients, current clients, and colleagues to your follow-up list whenever you get or meet them. Keep all clients on your targeted follow-up list.

Key Takeaways

Here's a quick summary of the key takeaways from Step 10:

- Up to 90% of the time, prospects aren't ready to hire a freelancer when you first contact them. Following up regularly with clients who expressed interest in your services but didn't need freelance help right away is an easy way to get more clients.

- Targeted follow-up with inactive and current clients and colleagues, especially other freelancers, also helps you get more freelance work.

- With fewer clients hiring freelancers in a recession, targeted follow-up is more important than ever. Targeted follow-up is professional and relevant.

- Once you get organized and develop your targeted follow-up process, a few hours a month can help you get more clients.

- Treat targeted follow-up like it's a deadline for a client. Get it done.

Congratulations! Finishing this book is your first step in being a fearless freelancer and thriving in a recession.

Become a Fearless Freelancer

Now you know that you can thrive in a recession. High-paying clients who regularly need the help of freelancers are still out there. You can get your share of these clients if you:

- Believe in yourself
- Adapt to the new normal
- Develop client-focused marketing tools and consistently market your freelance business.

In a sea of freelancers, client-focused marketing will make you stand out. You'll be able to get steady, high-paying clients and build a stable, successful freelance business. And you'll become a fearless freelancer.

Fearless Freelancers Work Hard

It won't be easy. You will have to work hard. But you won't waste your time or effort because the proven process in *The Fearless Freelancer* is based on what works best for freelancers.

Even in good times, doing a lot of marketing focused on how you help clients meet their needs pays off. That's how I built my freelance writing business to 6 figures in 18 months. And how I've been able to thrive in two recessions (and so far in my third recession), and continued to make 6 figures every year since 1998.

Doing a lot of marketing is more important than ever in a recession. Use the **Bonus Content for Fearless Freelancers** to develop and do your marketing. The bonus content includes dozens of checklists, templates, other tools, and blog posts to help you thrive in a recession.

A Special Offer to Help You Thrive

The Fearless Freelancer and the bonus content give you everything you need to market your freelance business and thrive in the recession.

But it's hard to do this on your own. If you want some help, consider my seven-week online course, **Finding the Freelance**

Clients You Deserve. The course covers the same content as this book, but you also get:

- Examples and more templates and other resources to help you apply what you're learning
- Assignments that guide you through each step.

Build Confidence and Marketing Skills with Coaching

You can take the course with or without coaching. In the coaching version, I provide advice based on your freelance business and answer your questions. Coaching includes before and after marketing reviews, key assignment reviews, two conference calls, and answers to questions about marketing your business via email.

Get on the VIP List for the Next Session

To learn more about the course, and get on the VIP list for the next session, email me at themightymarketer@comcast.net. Write "Yes, I want to thrive" in the subject line. I'll send you a link to more information about Finding the Freelance Clients You Deserve.

And I'll put you on the VIP list for the next session. If you decide you'd like to take the course, you'll be able to enroll before it fills up.

About the Author

Lori is a freelance writer who helps other freelancers use marketing to get the clients they deserve in good times and in bad.

When Lori started out, she didn't know anything about marketing. She made a lot of mistakes back then, like marketing to the wrong clients. The truth is, Lori didn't know which clients would hire her or what she could do for them. So she wasted a lot of time marketing to clients who would never hire her, because she didn't have the skills or experience they were looking for.

But because Lori did a lot of marketing in the first year or so, she was able to become a 6-figure freelancer in 18 months. And she was working with steady, high-paying clients who treated her right. Lori has been a 6-figure freelancer since 1998—including during three recessions.

As she met other freelancers, Lori noticed that many freelancers didn't know much about marketing and weren't comfortable doing it. So she began teaching them how to get the clients they deserve, through presentations, webinars, her Freelance Success blog, books, and online courses.

Now she's on a quest to help as many freelancers as possible become Mighty Marketers and build stable, successful freelance businesses. Born and raised in Philadelphia, Lori studied journalism at Temple University. She lives in South Jersey.

TheMightyMarketer.com

Bonus Content for Fearless Freelancers

Checklists, templates, other tools, and blog posts to help you thrive in a recession.

Get all bonus content:
www.themightymarketer.com/bonus-fearless-freelancer

Step 1. Develop the Fearless Freelancer Mindset

Blog post: The Superhero Power You Need to Know About: Grit

Blog post: How to Boost Your Resilience When Things Go Wrong

Blog post: 11 Ways to Keep Anxiety at Bay and Focus on Freelancing

Step 2. Stand Out in a Sea of Freelancers

Blog post: Case Studies: How 3 Freelancers Created Their Brands

Blog post: 11 Steps to a Business Name that Will Make You Memorable

Tool: Freelance Brand Statement Template

Step 3. Build the Marketing Habit

Blog post: The Habit that Will Make You a Success—Even in a Recession

Blog post: The Ultimate Guide to Goals for Freelance Success

Step 4. Choose Your Moneymaking Specialty(ies)

Tool: Simple Strategic Plan for Surviving the Recession

Blog post: Want to Worry Less and Make More Money? Be a Specialist

Step 5. Find the Right Prospects

Tool: Prospect List Template

Step 6. Reach and Attract the Right Clients with Direct Email

Tool: Direct Email Swipe File, with templates and examples

Step 7. Develop a Client-Focused LinkedIn Profile

Checklist: The Ultimate LinkedIn Profile Checklist for Freelancers

Guide: The Ultimate Guide to LinkedIn for Freelancers

Step 8. Create a Client-Focused Website

Checklist: Awesome Freelance Website Checklist

Blog post: How to Make Your Web Content Awesome, with Free Checklist

Tool: Awesome Freelance Website Template

Blog post: Why You Need a Website Designer

Step 9. Meet People Who Can Help and Hire You

Blog post: 3 Surefire Ways Volunteering Helps You Get Freelance Work

Tool: The Ultimate Networking Event Checklist for Freelancers

Blog post: 12 Ways to Make Networking Events Amazing, Not Scary

Blog post: How to Be Active and Effective on LinkedIn Even if You Hate Social Media

Step 10. Be First in Line for Freelance Work

Blog post: The Surprising Thing that Will Get You More Freelance Work: Follow-Up

Blog post: 11 Steps to a Remarkable E-Newsletter that Will Impress Clients

Blog post: Why You Need to Have an Email Newsletter

Tool: Targeted Follow-Up Tracker Template

Lightning Source UK Ltd.
Milton Keynes UK
UKHW020348061221
395149UK00005B/44

9 781647 187958